D1709416

COMPLEXITY CLASSIFICATIONS OF BOOLEAN CONSTRAINT SATISFACTION PROBLEMS

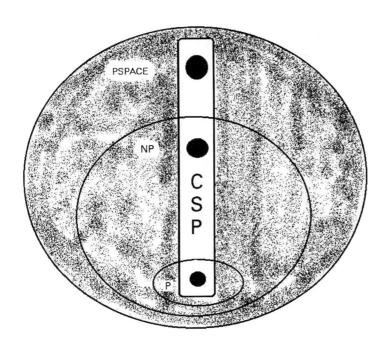

SIAM Monographs on Discrete Mathematics and Applications

The series includes advanced monographs reporting on the most recent theoretical, computational, or applied developments in the field; introductory volumes aimed at mathematicians and other mathematically motivated readers interested in understanding certain areas of pure or applied combinatorics; and graduate textbooks. The volumes are devoted to various areas of discrete mathematics and its applications.

Mathematicians, computer scientists, operations researchers, computationally oriented natural and social scientists, engineers, medical researchers, and other practitioners will find the volumes of interest.

Series Volumes

Creignou, N., Khanna, S., and Sudan, M., *Complexity Classifications of Boolean Constraint Satisfaction Problems*

Hubert, L., Arabie, P., and Meulman, J., *Combinatorial Data Analysis: Optimization by Dynamic Programming*

Peleg, D., *Distributed Computing: A Locality-Sensitive Approach*

Wegener, I., *Branching Programs and Binary Decision Diagrams: Theory and Applications*

Brandstädt, A., Le, V. B., and Spinrad, J. P., *Graph Classes: A Survey*

McKee, T. A. and McMorris, F. R., *Topics in Intersection Graph Theory*

Grilli di Cortona, P., Manzi, C., Pennisi, A., Ricca, F., and Simeone, B., *Evaluation and Optimization of Electoral Systems*

COMPLEXITY CLASSIFICATIONS OF BOOLEAN CONSTRAINT SATISFACTION PROBLEMS

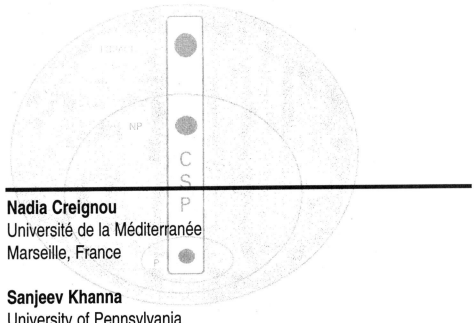

Nadia Creignou
Université de la Méditerranée
Marseille, France

Sanjeev Khanna
University of Pennsylvania
Philadelphia, Pennsylvania

Madhu Sudan
Massachusetts Institute of Technology
Cambridge, Massachusetts

siam.

Society for Industrial and Applied Mathematics
Philadelphia

Library of Congress Cataloging-in-Publication Data

Creignou, Nadia.
    Complexity classifications of Boolean constraint satisfaction problems / Nadia Creignou, Sanjeev Khanna, Madhu Sudan.
        p. cm. — (SIAM monographs on discrete mathematics and applications)
    Includes bibliographical references and index.
    ISBN 0-89871-479-6
        1. Computational complexity. 2. Constraints (Artificial intelligence) 3. Boolean algebra. I. Khanna, Sanjeev. II. Sudan, Madhu. III. Title. IV. Series.

QA267.7.C74 2001
511.3–dc21

00-050988

siam is a registered trademark.

Contents

Preface

This book presents a nearly complete classification of various restricted classes of computational problems called *Boolean constraint satisfaction problems*. Roughly, these are problems whose instances describe a collection of simple constraints on Boolean variables. A typical goal would be to find a setting to the Boolean variables that satisfies all the constraints. Variants of the problem may make the goal determining if such a setting exists, or counting the number of such settings or determining the "optimal" setting among those that satisfy all constraints, etc. This book studies all such problems and presents complexity results classifying them.

Constraint satisfaction problems are interesting in their own right. They occur commonly in practice, in optimization and in settings arising from artificial intelligence. This book presents a compact collection of rules that classify *every* constraint satisfaction problem as "easy" or "hard". Such a compact and complete classification of these problems has obvious utility to the practitioners that encounter such problems. The fact that there are infinitely many constraint satisfaction problems hints that the practitioner is likely to encounter a new one every once in a while. The typical researcher at this stage would either end up chasing references in a library or attempt to (re)solve this new computational problem: this book offers an alternative to these paths. It offers a calculus, or a guidebook of rules, that characterizes the complexity of this new problem and its numerous variants, while also presenting the best possible algorithm for solving this problem!

Such a calculus characterizing the complexity of computational problems is obviously of interest to "complexity theory" — the area that studies the computational complexity of solving mathematical problems. Complexity theory studies the complexity of solving any/every computational problem. The focus of this book may be considered a restriction of this goal — it focuses its attention on a restricted subclass of all problems.

The natural question to ask at this stage is: Why focus on a restricted class when one could study complexity theory in its full generality? The reason is that complexity theory is so general that its results become too weak. In its full scope, complexity theory easily possesses the ability to study itself, and therein subjects itself to the problem of diagonalization. This problem soon manifests itself everywhere. It suggests it is not possible to come up with simple rules saying when a problem is "easy" or "hard". (This is merely one of the many disastrous implications of a well-known theorem of Rice.) It blinds us from seeing evident generalizations of known principles, such as when a seemingly general technique (an algorithm or a hardness result) can be applied to a whole class of problems. As a consequence, most results are presented in isolated form — addressing one problem at a time.

This is where Boolean constraint satisfaction problems come to our rescue. They are not too general, so they don't succumb to diagonalization arguments; thus, a complete classification is not necessarily infeasible. And as we will show in this book, such a classification indeed exists and can be derived fairly easily. However, existence of the classification alone does not provide sufficient motivation to read about it. After all, if one restricts the class of problems sufficiently, a classification should not be hard! So to justify the restriction we still need to say why constraint satisfaction problems are of interest to the complexity theorist: this is easy. Take any of the standard texts on complexity and the first problem that is shown to be the canonical (complete) representative for a given class is typically a constraint satisfaction problem. Constraint satisfaction problems thus form the nucleus of many complexity classes, and could be interpreted to be the combinatorial core of complexity. This realization has been implicit to the researchers in complexity theory for several decades now and is brought out explicitly in this book. This book studies the restriction of many different complexity classes to constraint satisfaction problems. It unifies the techniques used to analyze all the different variants and formally justifies the many coincidences that were often observed about computation in the past.

Above, we have described two potential audiences for this book: Researchers in optimization/computer science who spend a good deal of their time analyzing new computational problems, for whom this book could be a handy reference, and researchers in complexity theory and discrete mathematics. There are many reasons for which the audience in the latter category may choose to read this book. The results presented here are a compact description of a large body of results proven in numerous papers. Moreover, the proofs presented here are often simpler than the ones presented in the original papers. But we view these as the secondary reasons to read this book. The primary reason is to learn about the potential importance of Boolean constraint satisfaction problems to their own area of work. These problems are an excellent testbed for abstracting some "global" inferences about the nature of computation, and may provide very useful hints at some hidden truths.

This book is intended for researchers and graduate students pursuing theoretical computer science or discrete mathematics. It was written with an awareness that the audience described above need not always share a common language or definitions. Thus we have attempted to keep the book as self-contained as possible. It is our hope that any reader who has taken the first course on the "Theory of Computation" should be in a position to follow the text fully. Comments from the readers on this or other aspects of the book (via email to `creignou@lim.univ-mrs.fr`, `sanjeev@cis.upenn.edu` or `madhu@mit.edu`) will be most welcome.

Nadia Creignou
Sanjeev Khanna
Madhu Sudan

Chapter 1

Introduction

One of the fundamental goals of the theory of computation, or "complexity theory", is to determine how much of a computational resource is required to solve a given computational task. Along the way it postulates definitions of when a task is computationally "easy" and when it is, or is likely to be, "hard". One of the modern definitions of computational "easiness" or "tractability" is that the task be solvable in time polynomial in the size of the input to the problem. A task is said to be "intractable" if there does not exist a polynomial time algorithm to solve it. While these definitions are straightforward, it turns out to be a highly challenging problem to explicitly classify a given computational task as tractable or not. In fact, for a wide variety of problems, of very differing flavor, this classification task remains open. (The famed "P = NP?" question is an example of such a classification question.)

In the face of this difficulty in establishing concrete lower bounds on the computational complexity of given problems, complexity theory has focused much of its attention on establishing a partial order among the problems in terms of computational difficulty. Crucial to this partial order is a computational mechanism, called "reduction", that shows one problem is at least as hard as another. Informally, a reduction metamorphoses a given computational problem into another, using only a bounded amount of computational resources, say, in polynomial time. If there exists a reduction from one problem to another, then this shows that the starting problem is tractable if the end-problem is tractable; or stated in the contrapositive, the end-problem is at least as hard as the starting problem. Using the notion of reductions, complexity theory has established a rich partial order among computational problems. Even more significantly, it has discovered a rich collection of equivalence classes of computational problems — each class contains numerous seemingly unrelated problems that turn out, however, to be computationally equivalent. These equivalence classes, commonly studied under the label of "completeness in complexity classes", capture innumerable phenomena that are uniquely computational in nature — phenomena that may have been easily overlooked if the computational restrictions were ignored, which yet play a fundamental role in computer science as well as human thought and reasoning. Examples of such phenomena include the complexity of searching a maze, the complexity of playing games, the complexity of enumerating solutions to a search problem, the complexity of finding the "best" solution to a search problem, complexity of computing with limited space or even the complexity of determining the complexity of a given problem! Arising from such phenomena are a host of exciting complexity classes such as NP, PSPACE, #P, MAX SNP, LOGSPACE and NC. These classes are formally introduced in Chapter 2.

1

The above mentioned list of complexity classes is by no means exhaustive. In fact, complexity theory deals with infinitely many complexity classes, infinitely many questions and deals with innumerable possible resolutions to these questions. It inherits these features from the fact that it places no limits on the kind of computational problems it deals with. Any problem that can be formally specified is included in its scope. This powerful feature, however, can also be a severely limiting factor in its scope! It limits the ability to present results compactly — the results are too diverse to allow any compact presentation. In order to meaningfully reason about infinitely many problems we need to be able to group them into a small number of classes. Unfortunately, there is a limited scope for unification, and it is hard to make universal statements about the behavior of natural problems. Specifically, there is an intriguing result of Ladner [64] that shows that if P $\neq$ NP, then there exist infinitely many equivalence classes between P and NP. Further, a well-known theorem of Rice says that it is undecidable to determine if a given problem is in P or not. Thus, these limitations are not mere perceptions, but rather formally proven barriers.

This monograph attempts to break free of these inherent barriers in the study of complexity theory by restricting its attention to a "microcosmos" of computational problems; namely, Boolean constraint satisfaction problems. We will define these shortly, and then see that this restricted class of problems continues to exhibit much of the natural diversity of computational problems without exhibiting the corresponding limitations. In particular, we will see that it is possible to define the Boolean constraint satisfaction version of the complexity classes NP, PSPACE, #P, MAX SNP, NC, etc.; these classes continue to have a rich collection of complete problems which are actually complete for the whole class (and not just for the restriction). The classes continue to have infinitely many different problems. However, it turns out that it is possible to completely classify the complexity of all the problems in these classes. And even though there are infinitely many problems in these classes whose computational complexity is not completely resolved, it turns out that there are only finitely many questions that are independent, and only finitely many possible resolutions to these questions. Thus, by focusing on this restricted world, it is possible to present a reasonably accurate bird's eye view of complexity theory and the equivalence classes it has created; and this is precisely what this monograph is intended to do.

1.1   Constraint satisfaction problems

We introduce constraint satisfaction problems informally by describing the prototypical example, namely, 3-SAT. This problem arises from the area of Boolean logic. An instance of 3-SAT is a "formula" $\phi = \phi(x_1, \ldots, x_n)$ defined on n Boolean variables $x_1, \ldots, x_n$. Each variable can be assigned either the value 0 (associated with the logical value "false") or the value 1 (associated with "true"). The n variables implicitly define $2n$ *literals* $l_1, \ldots, l_{2n}$, with the literal l_{2i-1} being associated with the variable x_i and the literal l_{2i} being associated with the negation of the variable x_i (the negation being denoted by $\neg x_i$ or $\bar{x}_i$). An assignment to the variables induces an assignment to the literals in a natural way: $l_{2i-1} = x_i$, while $l_{2i} = \neg x_i$. A clause $C = C(x_1, \ldots, x_n)$ is a disjunction of some k literals: $C = l_{i_1} \vee \cdots \vee l_{i_k}$. The clause C is satisfied by some assignment to the variables $x_1, \ldots, x_n$ if at least one of the literals $l_{i_1}, \ldots, l_{i_k}$ is set to 1 (or "true"). The length of the clause C is defined to be k. The formula ϕ then is the conjunction of some integer number, m, of "clauses" $C_1, \ldots, C_m$, each of length at most 3. (More generally, the k-SAT problem has as its instances, formulae in which each clause has length at most k.) The formula ϕ is said to be satisfied by an assignment to the variables $x_1, \ldots, x_n$ if every clause in ϕ is satisfied by the assignment. A formula ϕ is said to be satisfiable if it is satisfied by some assignment.

The computational problem 3-SAT is that of deciding if a given formula ϕ is satisfiable or not. No polynomial time algorithms (i.e., running in time that is bounded by a fixed polynomial in n and m) are known for this problem. This may come as a surprise to those unfamiliar with this problem; however it turns out that there is overwhelming belief today that such an algorithm may not exist. This belief is in turn equivalent to the conjecture "NP $\neq$ P", as was shown by the seminal result, obtained independently by Cook [14] and Levin [65], showing that "3-SAT is NP-complete", i.e., 3-SAT is actually as hard as any problem in NP.

One view of the 3-SAT problem is that it lays down a collection of "simple constraints" on n variables. Each clause C_j is a "constraint" in that it rules out certain assignments to the variables $x_1, \ldots, x_n$. These constraints are "simple" in that one can easily verify if a given assignment satisfies a given constraint: simply inspect the values assigned to the 3 variables. Yet, the NP-completeness of 3-SAT (and the associated belief that NP $\neq$ P) indicates that by stringing together m constraints of this simple form, one obtains a computational problem that is surprisingly hard. A natural question at this point would be: What aspect of the definition of the 3-SAT problem led to this computational hardness? Is it simply an artifact of stringing together a large number of constraints or is there something specific about the constraints (the clauses) of 3-SAT that forced this to happen?

It turns out that there *is* something special in the nature of the constraints of 3-SAT that makes this a computationally hard problem. This point is perhaps best illustrated by contrasting it with the classical 2-SAT problem. This is just the restriction of 3-SAT to instances in which every clause is of length at most 2. A folklore result shows that the 2-SAT problem is actually solvable in polynomial time.

Somewhat further away from the logical setting of 3-SAT is the problem of solving linear equations over GF(2). Notice that the Boolean variables $x_1, \ldots, x_n$ could be easily interpreted as elements of the finite field on two elements, with addition and multiplication being performed modulo 2. Thus one can define a constraint satisfaction problem motivated by this algebraic setting. Each constraint is now a linear constraint on some k variables and our goal is to determine if there exists an assignment satisfying all the linear constraints. Using the fact that Gaussian elimination works over any field, we see that this problem is also solvable efficiently, in time $O((m+n)^3)$.[1]

In view of the three examples above, it becomes clear that constraint satisfaction problems are neither trivially easy nor trivially hard. This motivates the topic of this monograph and our starting point is the work of Schaefer [82]. The broad nature of this (and subsequent works) is to study the complexity of deciding satisfiability of a given constraint satisfaction problem as a function of the "nature" of the constraint. To this end, Schaefer defined an infinite class of computational problems, which he referred to as the "generalized satisfiability problems." Informally speaking, a problem in this class is characterized by a finite collection of finitely specified constraint templates,[2] say, $\mathcal{F}$. An instance of such a problem, called the SAT($\mathcal{F}$) problem, consists of n Boolean variables and m constraints applied to various subsets of the given variables such that each constraint is drawn from the

---

[1]This may be a good time to remind the reader of the big-Oh notation: For functions $f(\cdot)$ and $g(\cdot)$ mapping positive integers to the positive integers, we say $f = O(g)$ if there exist $c, n_0 < \infty$ such that $f(n) \leq cg(n)$ for all $n \geq n_0$. The big-Oh notation allows for easy but approximate computations between growth of functions. We will be using this notation extensively.

[2]For the most part we will not care how these constraints are specified. A canonical assumption would be that a constraint is specified by a truth table. In Chapter 9 we will describe some other natural representations for specifying constraints.

collection $\mathcal{F}$. The objective is to determine if there is an assignment to the input variables which satisfies all the given constraints.

Schaefer was interested in studying the complexity of answering the above question for every problem in the class. His study led to a strikingly simple answer: every problem in this class is either in P or is NP-complete. Moreover, there is a concise characterization that allows us to determine whether for a given $\mathcal{F}$, $\mathsf{SAT}(\mathcal{F})$ is in P or is NP-complete.

Schaefer's result is surprising and unexpected for several reasons. First, prior to this result, NP-completeness proofs were established on a problem by problem basis. Schaefer's result gave a uniform proof to establish NP-completeness of an infinite collection of problems. Second, rarely in complexity theory does one comes across an infinite class of problems where every problem belongs to a finite collection of (computational) equivalence classes. The above mentioned result of Ladner had ruled out this possibility if P $\neq$ NP. Finally, the result comes with a compact collection of classification rules, which tell when a problem is in P and when it is NP-complete. This also overcomes the hurdle posed by Rice's theorem!

Recent research in complexity theory has tried to generalize and extend Schaefer's results in several ways. In one direction, Feder and Vardi [28] study generalized satisfiability problems when the variables in the domain are not restricted to being Boolean, but allowed to take on any one of finitely many values. They refer to their problems as Constraint Satisfaction Problems; and we inherit this name from their work. The simple change of allowing non-Boolean variables seems to increase the expressive power of the constraint satisfaction problems considerably. Feder and Vardi raise the question of whether the dichotomy exhibited in the Boolean case continues to hold in the non-Boolean case. Surprisingly, this turns out to be a much harder question and remains unresolved to this date. However Feder and Vardi prove a number of interesting facts about constraint satisfaction problems including that this may be the largest subclass of NP (where largest is meant to be interpreted carefully) that exhibits a dichotomy. Since many central questions surrounding non-Boolean constraint satisfaction problems remain unresolved, we shall only focus on Boolean "constraint satisfaction problems" in this monograph.

There is a growing body of classification results for problems derived from Boolean constraint satisfaction. These results extend Schaefer's study and explore different kinds of complexity classes restricted to constraint satisfaction problems. This direction of research includes the works of Creignou [17], Kavvadias and Sideri [51], Creignou and Hermann [19] Creignou and Hébrard [18], Khanna and Sudan [54], Khanna, Sudan and Williamson [56], Khanna, Sudan and Trevisan [55], Reith and Vollmer [80]. Together they have shown classification results for a variety of computational tasks, where the goal of the computation varies while the instance of the problem remains the same. Some specific results in this sequence include the following. Creignou [17] and Khanna and Sudan [54] independently studied optimization problems where the objective is to maximize the number of satisfied constraints in a given instance of a constraint satisfaction problem. They show that every optimization problem in this class is either in P or APX-complete. Kavvadias and Sideri [51] studied the inverse satisfiability problem where the goal is to construct a collection of constraint applications such that a given set of truth assignments constitutes its set of feasible solutions. They show dichotomy results for this class of problems. Creignou and Hermann [19] show a FP/#P-complete dichotomy for counting versions of constraint satisfaction problems where the objective is to count the number of assignments satisfying all constraints. Creignou and Hébrard [18] show a dichotomy with respect to the complexity of enumerating all satisfying solutions. Reith and Vollmer [80] have studied a class of optimization problems where the objective is to find a lexicographically minimal (or maximal) satisfying assignment. Khanna et al. [56, 55] study other forms of commonly occurring optimization tasks in the constraint satisfiability setting and obtain classification results. The results of Khanna et al. [56, 55] are somewhat different from the others above in that the resulting classification theorems do not exhibit dichotomies but rather give a partition into a larger but finite number of equivalence classes.

1.2 Organization

This monograph is a uniform survey of these results: results that we refer to as classification results on constraint satisfaction problems. En route, we present some new classification results and a refinement of many of these results. We now describe the layout of this monograph. Chapters 2 and 3 give some of the introductory material associated with our theme. Chapter 2 gives a (very) brief summary of some of the common complexity classes and related reductions. Chapter 3 formally introduces constraint satisfaction problems and shows how the classes introduced in Chapter 2 can be studied in this restricted setting.

Chapter 4 initiates the technical study of constraint satisfaction problems. It describes some broad divisions among families of constraints and shows some preliminary properties or "characterizations" of constraint families. Recall that our eventual goal is to present results of the form: "If all constraints in a given set of templates $\mathcal{F}$ satisfy a certain property $\mathcal{P}$, then a canonical algorithm can be applied to solve the problem efficiently. The absence of the property $\mathcal{P}$ can be used to show that solving the constraint satisfaction problem associated with $\mathcal{F}$ is hard."[3] A first step in this direction is to express succinctly what properties are exhibited by a family $\mathcal{F}$, if it does *not* satisfy a property $\mathcal{P}$. This is the focus of Chapter 4.

Chapter 5 is the central chapter of this monograph and focuses on a unifying theme among reductions between constraint satisfaction problems. One of the surprising aspects of dealing with constraint satisfaction problems is that even though there exist so many different variations of the main theme, the tools used for dealing with them are essentially the same. In fact, a similar view could be expressed of complexity theory in general; however, this would be more contentious. In our case, we can actually "prove" this assertion. We introduce in Chapter 5 a notion of how a family of constraints may be used to "implement" other constraints. We show that this one definition captures reducibility among constraint satisfaction problems, almost independent of the actual theme (be it decision, counting, enumeration or optimization). We then go on to show how the characterizations of Chapter 4 can be used to build a basic toolkit of implementations.

In the following chapters, we repeatedly employ this basic toolkit to analyze different classes of constraint satisfaction problems. Chapter 6 presents dichotomy results for decision, counting, space complexity, and parallel complexity. Chapter 7 presents classification results for optimization problems.

One of the somewhat disappointing conclusions of the study of constraint satisfaction problems is that too many problems turn out to be hard. One possible reason for this is that instances typically have no restrictions on how the variables interact with the constraints. In Chapter 8 we show that, even for studying such limitations of constraint satisfaction problems, the best formal approach appears to be via constraint satisfaction. We show how

---

[3]This is in the spirit of Post's classic theorem which gives a characterization of all families $\mathcal{F}$ that form complete bases for all Boolean functions.

natural restrictions such as planarity and density can be expressed naturally in this context; and further lead to tractability results for otherwise intractable problems.

Finally, in Chapter 9 we go up one level in the nature of questions asked. We focus on a computational version of the questions tackled in Chapter 4. It asks: "What is the complexity of determining if a given family $\mathcal{F}$ satisfies a property $\mathcal{P}$?" Note that this question is relevant to the complexity of evaluating the classification rules presented in Chapters 6 and 7. Naturally an answer to this question depends on the representation of $\mathcal{F}$. Chapter 9 answers this question for several natural representations.

To conclude this chapter, we would like to point out that while our framework of "constraint satisfaction problems" allows us to take a unified look at complexity theory, this is by no means the only such framework. We are aware of several other families of classification results that are not covered by our study. Examples of such results include: classification results for the directed subgraph homeomorphism problem due to Fortune, Hopcroft and Wyllie [30]; classification results for the H-coloring problem on graphs due to Hell and Nesetril [37]; classification results on graph decomposition due to Dor and Tarsi [24]; classification results for vertex deletion problems on monotone graph properties due to Lund and Yannakakis [70]. Even within the scope of constraint satisfaction problems, our approach using implementations is not the only successful one. An alternate approach due to Boros *et al* [11] uses a linear programming based approach to measure the complexity of satisfiability problems. We shall not, however, expand our scope to include these alternate approaches. We shall remained focused on the approach via Boolean constraint satisfaction problems, and hope to highlight its simple unifying view of complexity theory.

Chapter 2

Complexity Classes

Here we present a quick review of the various complexity classes that arise in the course of our study. We describe three basic forms of computational tasks: Decision problems, Counting problems and Optimization problems. In each case we describe some central complexity classes. This includes the classical complexity classes such as P, NP and PSPACE; some more recent ones such as NC and #P; and some very modern ones such as PO and NPO (the last ones arising from the study of the approximability of optimization problems). We then define notions of completeness for each complexity class, by introducing appropriate notions of reducibility. These definitions form the backdrop for our study of Boolean constraint satisfaction problems to be introduced in Chapter 3, where we will specialize all these classes to the case of Boolean constraint satisfaction problems.

Our definitions rely on some well-known formalisms of models of computation. The most commonly used models will be those of deterministic and non-deterministic Turing machines and sometimes the notion of random access machines (see, for instance, [12], [39], [75], or [84]). Other models of computation we rely on include uniform Boolean (and arithmetic) circuits families (see, for instance, [36]).

2.1 Decision problems

Decision problems are the simplest forms of computational tasks in which the goal of the computation is to "decide" if a given input satisfies as given property (or lies in a given language). Formally, a *decision problem* Π is a function that takes as input a string over a finite alphabet Σ and maps it to one of the two possible answers, "yes" or "no". A *language* is any subset of Σ^*. There is a natural correspondence between decision problems and languages. Given a decision problem Π, we can associate with it a language $L_\Pi \subset \Sigma^*$ which consists of all strings that are mapped to "yes" by the problem Π. From here on, we will work with the languages derived from the decision problems.

2.1.1 The classes P, NP, coNP, PSPACE

Let f be a function whose domain and range are non-negative integers. We define below the notion of languages belonging to a time or space complexity class.

Definition 2.1 [DTIME($f(n)$) and DSPACE($f(n)$)] *The complexity class* DTIME($f(n)$) DSPACE($f(n)$) *is the class of all languages accepted by a deterministic Turing machine* *within time (space) $f(n)$.*

We can also define time and space complexity classes with non-deterministic Turing machines.

Definition 2.2 [NTIME($f(n)$) and NSPACE($f(n)$)] *The complexity class* NTIME($f(n)$) NSPACE($f(n)$) *is the class of all languages accepted by a non-deterministic Turing machine within time (space) $f(n)$.*

Definition 2.3 [P] *The class of languages accepted in polynomial time by a deterministic Turing machine is denoted by* P*:*

$$P = \bigcup_k DTIME(n^k).$$

Definition 2.4 [NP] *The class of languages accepted in polynomial time by a non-deterministic Turing machine is denoted by* NP*:*

$$NP = \bigcup_k NTIME(n^k).$$

Taking the union over all exponents k ensures that these classes are stable and robust with respect to variations in the underlying computational model (see [75]). For instance, P is also the class of problems decidable in polynomial time by a random access machine.

There is an alternative, and perhaps more natural, way of viewing the class NP. One can define NP as the class of languages whose members have short, easily verifiable proofs. The easy verifiability property is formalized via a polynomial time computable binary relation R, and the NP language consists of all strings x for which there exists a short *proof y* (also called *certificate* or *witness*) such that $R(x, y)$ holds. We formalize this below.

Definition 2.5 *Let $R \subseteq \Sigma^* \times \Sigma^*$ be a binary relation. The relation R is a p-*predicate *if there exist two polynomials p and q such that:*

- $\forall (x, y) \in \Sigma^* \times \Sigma^*,\ R(x, y)$ *implies* $|y| \leq p(|x|)$,

- $\forall (x, y) \in \Sigma^* \times \Sigma^*,\ R(x, y)$ *is decidable in time* $q(|x|)$.

Proposition 2.6 *Let $L \subseteq \Sigma^*$ be a language. Then $L \in$ NP if and only if there exists a p-predicate R such that*

$$L = \{x \mid R(x, y) \text{ for some } y\}.$$

Thus, intuitively speaking, the difference between P and NP is akin to the difference between efficiently finding a proof of a statement and efficiently verifying a proof.

Analogous to the time complexity classes P and NP, we can define the space complexity classes PSPACE and NPSPACE.

Definition 2.7 [PSPACE and NPSPACE] *The class of languages accepted in polynomial space by a deterministic (non-deterministic) Turing machine is denoted by* PSPACE (NPSPACE)*:*

$$PSPACE = \bigcup_k DSPACE(n^k), \text{ and}$$

$$NPSPACE = \bigcup_k NSPACE(n^k).$$

While, for the time complexity, a fundamental unresolved question is whether P = NP, a classic result of Savitch long ago settled the analogous question for space complexity.

Proposition 2.8 [81] PSPACE = NPSPACE.

Definition 2.9 *For any complexity class $\mathcal{C}$, co$\mathcal{C}$ denotes the complement of class $\mathcal{C}$, given by the following set:*

$$co\mathcal{C} = \{\Sigma^* \setminus L \; : \; L \in \mathcal{C}\}.$$

It is easily seen that if $\mathcal{C}$ is a deterministic time or space complexity class, then $\mathcal{C} = co\mathcal{C}$. Thus, among the four complexity classes introduced above, it is only relevant to study the complement of the class NP, namely, the class *co*NP.

2.1.2 Reductions and NP and PSPACE completeness

Reductions play a central role in identifying the hardest problems in any complexity class. We now define the appropriate notion of reductions for the classes NP and PSPACE.

Definition 2.10 *We say that a language $L_1 \subset \Sigma_1^*$ is reducible to a language $L_2 \subset \Sigma_2^*$ if there is a function $f : \Sigma_1^* \longrightarrow \Sigma_2^*$ such that for all $x \in \Sigma_1^*$, $x \in L_1$ if and only if $f(x) \in L_2$. If the function f is computable in polynomial time by a deterministic Turing machine, we say that L_1 is polynomial-time reducible to L_2. Similarly, if the function f is computable in logarithmic space (that is, using $O(\log(|x|))$ cells on any storage tape) by a deterministic Turing machine, we say that L_1 is log-space reducible to L_2.*

Note that any log-space reduction is also a polynomial-time reduction.

Proposition 2.11 *The composition of two log-pace (polynomial-time) reductions is a log-space (polynomial-time) reduction.*

The significance of these reductions comes from the following lemmas.

Lemma 2.12 *If L_1 is polynomial-time reducible to L_2, then $L_2 \in$ P implies $L_1 \in$ P (and equivalently, $L_1 \notin$ P implies $L_2 \notin$ P).*

Lemma 2.13 *If L_1 is log-space reducible to L_2, then*

1. *$L_2 \in$ P implies $L_1 \in$ P,*

2. *$L_2 \in$ NSPACE($\log^k n$) implies $L_1 \in$ NSPACE($\log^k n$), and*

3. *$L_2 \in$ DSPACE($\log^k n$) implies $L_1 \in$ DSPACE($\log^k n$).*

We can now introduce the notion of complete problems for NP and PSPACE.

Definition 2.14 [NP-hard and NP-complete] *A language $L \subset \Sigma^*$ is NP-hard if every language L' in NP is polynomial-time reducible to L. If, in addition, L belongs to the class NP, we say that L is NP-complete.*

If L_1 is an NP-hard problem and there is a polynomial-time reduction from L_1 to L_2, then L_2 is an NP-hard problem. Observe that an NP-complete problem $\Pi \in$ P if and only if P = NP.

Example 2.15 *Consider the problem* SAT *defined below:*

    INSTANCE : *A Boolean CNF formula* Φ.

    OBJECTIVE : *Is there a truth assignment that satisfies* Φ?

SAT *is the first problem shown to be* NP-*complete* [14, 65].

There is a wide variety of other known NP-complete problems. We shall list some of them here.

- k-SAT (k $\geq$ 3):

  INSTANCE : A Boolean CNF formula Φ with k literals per clause.

  OBJECTIVE : Is there a truth assignment that satisfies Φ?

- VERTEX COVER:

  INSTANCE : A graph $G = (V, E)$ and a positive integer $K \leq |V|$.

  OBJECTIVE : Does V contain a vertex cover of size K or less, i.e., a subset $V' \subseteq V$ with $|V'| \leq K$ such that for each edge $\{u, v\}$ in E at least one of u and v belongs to V'.

- CLIQUE:

  INSTANCE : A graph $G = (V, E)$ and a positive integer $K \leq |V|$.

  OBJECTIVE : Does V contain a clique of size K or more, i.e., a subset $V' \subseteq V$ with $|V'| \geq K$ such that every pair of vertices in V' are joined by an edge in E?

- INDEPENDENT SET:

  INSTANCE : A graph $G = (V, E)$ and a positive integer $K \leq |V|$.

  OBJECTIVE : Does V contain an independent set of size K or more, i.e., a subset $V' \subseteq V$ with $|V'| \geq K$ such that no two vertices in V' are joined by an edge in E?

- GRAPH PARTITION:

  INSTANCE : A graph $G = (V, E)$, a weight $w(e) \in N$ for each $e \in E$ and a positive integer K.

  OBJECTIVE : Is there a partition into two disjoint sets V_1 and V_2 such that the sum of the weights of the edges from E that have one endpoint in V_1 and another endpoint in V_2, is at least K?

Polynomial-time reductions are also appropriate for defining coNP-completeness. Moreover, we have the following.

Proposition 2.16 *If* $L \in \Sigma^*$ *is* NP-*complete, then* $\bar{L} = \Sigma^* \setminus L$ *is* coNP-*complete.*

The problems that are coNP-complete are the least likely ones to be in class P, or for that matter, even in the class NP.

Proposition 2.17 *If a* coNP-*complete problem is in* NP, *then* NP = coNP.

PSPACE-completeness is defined using log-space reductions.

Definition 2.18 [PSPACE-hard and PSPACE-complete] *A language $L \subset \Sigma^*$ is* PSPACE-*hard if every language L' in* PSPACE *is log-space reducible to L. If in addition L is a member of* PSPACE, *then we say that L is* PSPACE-*complete.*

Example 2.19 *A representative* PSPACE *problem is the* QSAT *problem defined as below:*

INSTANCE : *A quantified formula $F = (Q_1 \; x_1)(Q_2 \; x_2) \ldots (Q_n \; x_n)\Phi$, where Φ is a CNF formula with Boolean variables $x_1, \ldots, x_n$ and Q_i is either the quantifier "for all" or "exists".*
OBJECTIVE : *Is F true?*

QSAT *is* PSPACE-*complete* [85].

2.1.3   Parallel complexity: The class NC and P-completeness

We now review the parallel complexity class NC as well as introduce P-complete problems, which are problems in P that are least likely to have fast parallel algorithms. The class NC consists of problems that are solvable in polylogarithmic time using only a polynomial number of processors. The formal definition below uses uniform Boolean circuits families (see [36, Chapter 2, Section 2.3.1, page 30]) as the underlying computational model.

Definition 2.20 [NC^k] *For each integer $k \geq 1$ the class NC^k is the set of all languages L such that L is recognized by a uniform Boolean circuits family $\{\alpha_n\}$ with $size(\alpha_n) = n^{O(1)}$ and $depth(\alpha_n) = O((\log n)^k)$.*

Definition 2.21 [NC] $\mathrm{NC} = \bigcup_k \mathrm{NC}^k$.

The class FNC is the set of all functions that are computable in polylogarithmic time using only polynomially many processors.

Example 2.22 *Matrix multiplication is in* FNC.

It is clearly the case that every problem in the class NC also belongs to the class P. However, an important open question is whether this inclusion is proper. As in the case of P versus NP question, complete problems have been identified — these are problems that are least likely to have NC algorithms. The notion of reductions used towards this end is that of log-space reductions.

Proposition 2.23 *If L is log-space reducible to L' and $L' \in \mathrm{NC}$, then $L \in \mathrm{NC}$.*

We can now define P-completeness.

Definition 2.24 [P-hard and P-complete] *A language L is P-hard if every language L' in P is log-space reducible to L. If, in addition, $L \in \mathrm{P}$, then we say that L is P-complete.*

Example 2.25 *Consider the problem of computing the maximum flow possible between two given points in a capacitated network.*

MAX FLOW*:*

INSTANCE : *A directed graph $G = (V, E)$, with each edge labeled by a capacity $c(e)$, two distinguished vertices source s and sink t, and a value f.*
OBJECTIVE : *Is there a flow of value f from s to t that does not violate any capacity constraints?*

MAX FLOW *is P-complete* [35].

2.2   Counting problems

We have so far studied decision problems where we wish to determine whether a feasible solution exists for a given input instance. A natural extension of this question is to determine the total number of feasible solutions for a given instance.

2.2.1   The class #P

Consider the following generalization of the SAT problem, referred to as #SAT:

> INSTANCE : A Boolean CNF formula Φ.

> OBJECTIVE : Compute the number of different truth assignments that satisfy Φ?

In general, for any NP language L, we can associate a counting problem $\#L(x) = \#\{y \mid R(x, y)\}$. We now define the class #P, the class of counting functions associated with NP problems.

Definition 2.26 [#P] *A function $F \colon \Sigma^* \to N$ is in* #P *if there is a p-predicate R such that for all $x \in \Sigma^*$, $F(x) = \#\{y \mid R(x, y)\}$.*

By the same token, FP denotes the class of functions $\Sigma^* \to N$ computable in deterministic polynomial time. Clearly, FP is a subclass of #P.

2.2.2   Parsimonious reductions and #P-completeness

Counting problems are related to one another via *counting reductions* and *parsimonious reductions*, which have stronger properties than the polynomial-time reductions used for NP problems.

Definition 2.27 [61] *Let $f, g \colon \Sigma^* \to N$ be two functions. A* polynomial many-one counting reduction (*or simply a* counting reduction) *from f to g consists of a pair of polynomial-time computable functions $\sigma \colon \Sigma^* \to \Sigma^*$ and $\tau \colon N \to N$ such that the equality $f(x) = \tau(g(\sigma(x)))$ holds. When such a reduction exists we say that f* reduces to *g. Such reductions are often called* weakly parsimonious. *A parsimonious reduction from f to g is a counting reduction σ, τ from f to g such that τ is the identity function.*

The reductions in the #P-hardness proofs must preserve the number of solutions and hence the necessity to look for parsimonious or weakly parsimonious reductions. Note that the (weakly) parsimonious reductions are closed under composition.

Definition 2.28 [#P-complete] *A counting problem $\#L$ is* #P-hard *if for every problem $\#L' \in$ #P there exists a counting reduction from $\#L'$ to $\#L$. If, in addition, $\#L$ is a member of* #P, *we say that the counting problem $\#L$ is* #P-complete.

If $\#L_1$ is a #P-complete problem and there is a counting reduction from $\#L_1$ to $\#L_2$, then $\#L_2$ is a #P-hard problem.

Example 2.29 *The* NP-*completeness proof for* SAT *can be adapted to show that* #SAT *is* #P-*complete.*

Even when a feasible solution to a problem can be found in polynomial time, the counting version of the problem can be #P-complete.

Example 2.30 *The decision problem* 2-SAT *is in* P *(see* [5]*, for instance) whereas the corresponding counting problem #2-SAT is #P-complete* [89].

It is generally believed that #P-hard problems are not members of the class FPH, the functional analog of the polynomial hierarchy PH. In particular, no #P-hard problem is known to belong to the class FP^{NP} of all functions that are computable in polynomial time using NP oracles [46, section 4.1]. In contrast, Toda [87] showed that the polynomial hierarchy is contained in the class $\text{P}^{\#\text{P}}$ of problems computable in polynomial time with the help of #P-oracles. Thus, to the extent that one can compare decision problems with counting problems, a #P-completeness result suggests a higher level of intractability than an NP-completeness result.

2.3 Optimization problems

A significant part of our study will be devoted to classifying the approximability of NP optimization problems (NPO). In this section we review some basic concepts related to approximability and describe the various approximation-preserving reductions that we will use. We start with a formal definition of the class NPO.

Definition 2.31 [NPO][45, 21] *An* NPO *problem (over a finite alphabet* Σ *) is a four-tuple* $\Pi = (\mathcal{I}, S, m, \text{OPT})$*, where*

- $\mathcal{I} \subseteq \Sigma^*$ *is the space of* input instances.

- $S(x) \subseteq \Sigma^*$ *is the space of* feasible solutions *on the input* $x \in \mathcal{I}$*. The only requirement on* S *is that there exists a p-predicate* R*, only depending on* Π*, such that for all* $x \in \mathcal{I}$*,* S *can be expressed as* $S(x) = \{y \mid R(x, y)\}$*.*

- $m: \mathcal{I} \times \Sigma^* \to N$*, the* objective function*, is a polynomial time computable function,* $m(x, y)$ *is defined only when* $y \in S(x)$*.*

- $\text{OPT} \in \{\max, \min\}$ *tells if* Π *is a* maximization *or a* minimization *problem.*

Solving an optimization problem Π given the input $x \in \mathcal{I}$ means finding a feasible solution $y \in S(x)$ such that $m(x, y)$ is optimal, that is as large as possible if $\text{OPT}_f = \max$ and as small as possible if $\text{OPT}_f = \min$. Let $\text{OPT}(x)$ denote this optimal value of m.

Many of the decision problems introduced in Section 2.1 were obtained from optimzation problems. Here we describe the underlying optimization problems related to CLIQUE, INDEPENDENT SET, k-SAT, VERTEX COVER, and GRAPH PARTITION. We start with MAX CLIQUE, the optimization version of CLIQUE, which is an example of an NPO maximization problem.

Example 2.32 MAX CLIQUE*:* INSTANCE *: A graph* $G = (V, E)$*.*
    OBJECTIVE *: Find the largest clique in* G*.*

Formally, MAX CLIQUE can be described by the tuple $(\mathcal{I}, S, m, \text{OPT})$, where the space $\mathcal{I}$ of input instances consists of all graphs G, the set of feasible solutions $S(G)$ is the set of cliques C of G, the objective function $m(G, C)$ is the cardinality of C, and $\text{OPT} = \max$.

Some of the other standard optimization problems are described below. We skip the straightforward translation that would show that these are NPO problems.

- MAX k-SAT:

  INSTANCE : A Boolean CNF formula Φ with m clauses, each having up to k literals per clause.

  OBJECTIVE : Find the truth assignment that satisfies the maximum number of clauses in Φ.

- MIN VERTEX COVER:

  INSTANCE : A graph $G = (V, E)$ and a collection of weights $w(u)$ for each $u \in V$.

  OBJECTIVE : Find a vertex cover C of the graph G that minimizes the sum of weights of vertices in C.

- MAX CUT:

  INSTANCE : A graph $G = (V, E)$ and a collection of weights $w(e) \in N$ for each $e \in E$.

  OBJECTIVE : Find a partition of V into V_1 and V_2 that maximizes the sum of the weight of edges with one endpoint each in V_1 and V_2.

Definition 2.33 PO *is the class of* NPO *problems that can be solved in polynomial time.*

Example 2.34 *The* s,t-MIN CUT *problem defined below is in* PO.

INSTANCE : *A graph $G = (V, E)$, weight $w(e)$ for each $e \in E$, specified vertices $s, t \in V$.*
OBJECTIVE : *Find a partition of V into two disjoint sets V_1 and V_2 such that $s \in V_1$, $t \in V_2$ so as to minimize the sum of the weights of the edges from E that have an endpoint in V_1 and one endpoint in V_2.*

2.3.1   Approximate solutions and approximation classes

Unless P = NP, there do not exist algorithms to compute optimal solutions to NP-hard optimization problems in polynomial time. It is then natural to consider a relaxed objective, namely, that of finding approximate solutions, i.e., solutions that are close to the optimal value but not necessarily optimal. Polynomial-time algorithms that do not necessarily compute an optimal solution for an underlying problem are referred to as *approximation algorithms*. As it turns out, NPO problems exhibit a very diverse behavior with respect to approximability. At one end of the spectrum, there are NP-hard optimization problems for which one can find in polynomial time solutions that are arbitrarily close to optimal. On the other hand, for many problems, it is NP-hard to even compute a solution that is only a polynomial factor away from the optimal. The goal of this section is to introduce some frequently arising approximability behaviors and the notion of approximation-preserving reductions.

Definition 2.35 [performance ratio] *An approximation algorithm for an* NPO *problem* Π *has* performance ratio $\mathcal{R}(n)$ *if, given an instance $x \in \mathcal{I}$ with $|x| = n$, it computes a solution $y \in S(x)$ which satisfies*

$$\max \left\{ \frac{m(x, y)}{\mathrm{OPT}(x)}, \frac{\mathrm{OPT}(x)}{m(x, y)} \right\} \leq \mathcal{R}(n).$$

A solution satisfying the above inequality is referred to as being $\mathcal{R}(n)$-*approximate*. We say that an NPO problem is *approximable to within a factor* $\mathcal{R}(n)$ if it has a polynomial-time approximation algorithm with performance ratio $\mathcal{R}(n)$.

An algorithm which approximates an NPO problem Π to within 1 by definition finds an optimal solution to the problem in polynomial time. For any NP-complete problem there is no such algorithm (unless P = NP). But for many NP-complete problems there are polynomial-time algorithms which approximate them to within $1 + \varepsilon$ for each $\varepsilon > 0$. Such an algorithm is called a *polynomial time approximation scheme* and is defined as follows.

Definition 2.36 [PTAS] *We say that an optimization problem Π has a polynomial time approximation scheme (PTAS) if there is a polynomial-time approximation algorithm that takes as input both an instance $x \in \mathcal{I}$ and a fixed parameter $\varepsilon > 0$, and outputs a solution which is $(1 + \varepsilon)$-approximate.*

Example 2.37 *The problem of finding a maximum independent set in a planar graph has a PTAS* [6].

Now we define three other kinds of approximability behaviors that frequently arise in the study of NPO problems.

Definition 2.38 [APX] *An NPO problem Π is in the class* APX *if there exists a polynomial-time algorithm for Π whose performance ratio is bounded by a constant.*

Example 2.39 *The optimization problem* MAX CUT *is in* APX.

Definition 2.40 [log-APX and poly-APX] *An NPO problem Π is in the class* log-APX *(poly-APX) if there exists a polynomial-time algorithm for Π whose performance ratio is bounded by a logarithmic factor (polynomial factor) in the size of the input.*

Example 2.41 *Let us consider the following two covering problems:*

HITTING SET-B

> INSTANCE : *A collection $\mathcal{C}$ of subsets of a finite set S, with $|c| \leq B$ for all $c \in \mathcal{C}$.*
> OBJECTIVE : *Find a subset $S' \subseteq S$ that contains at least one element from each subset in $\mathcal{C}$ such that $|S'|$ is minimum.*

MIN SET COVER

> INSTANCE : *A finite set X and $\mathcal{C}$ a collection of subsets of X which covers X.*
> OBJECTIVE : *Find a sub-collection $\mathcal{C}' \subseteq \mathcal{C}$ which also covers X such that $|\mathcal{C}'|$ is minimum.*

The problem HITTING SET-B *is in* APX *while* MIN SET COVER *is in* log-APX.

Example 2.42 *The problem* MAX CLIQUE *is in* poly-APX.

2.3.2 Approximation-preserving reductions and f-APX completeness

Completeness in approximation classes is defined via appropriate approximation-preserving reducibilities. There are two different types of approximation-preserving reducibilities that we will use in this work, namely, *A-reducibility* and *AP-reducibility*. The first of these below preserves a coarse level of approximability, while the latter is more fine in its preservation of approximability. The coarser definition is useful because it is easier to obtain such reductions; the finer one is needed when one is attempting to establish completeness at low levels of approximability (such as, say, for APX).

Definition 2.43 [A-reducibility] [21]   *An* NPO *problem* Π_1 *is said to be A-reducible to an* NPO *problem* Π_2, *denoted by* $\Pi_1 \leq_A \Pi_2$, *if two polynomial-time computable functions* f *and* g *and a constant* α *exist such that:*

1. *For any instance* x *of* Π_1, $x \in \mathcal{I}_1$, $f(x)$ *is an instance of* Π_2, $f(x) \in \mathcal{I}_2$.

2. *For any instance* $x \in \mathcal{I}_1$, *and for any feasible solution* y' *for* $f(x)$, $y' \in S_2(f(x))$, $g(x, y')$ *is a feasible solution for* x, $g(x, y') \in S_1(x)$.

3. *For any instance* x *of* Π_1, *and for any* $r > 1$, *if* y' *is an* r-approximate solution for $f(x)$, *then* $g(x, y')$ *is an* (αr)-approximate for x.

Definition 2.44 [AP-reducibility] [20]   *An* NPO *problem* Π_1 *is said to be AP-reducible to an* NPO *problem* Π_2, *denoted by* $\Pi_1 \leq_{AP} \Pi_2$, *if two polynomial-time computable functions* f *and* g *and a constant* α *exist such that*

1. *for any instance* x *of* Π_1, $x \in \mathcal{I}_1$, $f(x)$ *is an instance of* Π_2, $f(x) \in \mathcal{I}_2$.

2. *for any instance* x *of* Π_1, $x \in \mathcal{I}_1$, *and for any feasible solution* y' *for* $f(x)$, $y' \in S_2(f(x))$, $g(x, y')$ *is a feasible solution for* x, $g(x, y') \in S_1(x)$.

3. *for any instance* x *of* Π_1, *and for any* $r > 1$, *if* y' *is an* r-approximate solution for $f(x)$, *then* $g(x, y')$ *is a* $(1 + (r - 1)\alpha + o(1))$-approximate for x, *where the* o *notation is with respect to* $|x|$.

The main difference between the two reductions is in the item (3) of the definitions. The requirement in this item is more stringent for an AP-reduction and thus every AP-reduction is also an A-reduction, but not vice versa. Some elementary properties of the above reductions are illustrated below:

- If Π_1 is AP-reducible to Π_2 and Π_2 is in PTAS (resp., APX, log-APX or poly-APX), then so is Π_1.

- Let Π_1 be A-reducible to Π_2 with the function f, mapping instances of Π_1 to instances of Π_2, being computable in quadratic time. If Π_2 is approximable to within a factor $n^{1/3}$ (resp., $\log n$ or $(1 + \epsilon)$), then Π_1 is approximable to within a factor of $O(n^{2/3})$ (resp., $O(\log n)$ or $O(1 + \epsilon)$) time. Consequently, we have, if Π_2 is in poly-APX (resp., log-APX or APX) then so is Π_1. Note, however, that if Π_2 is in PO or PTAS, then Π_1 need not be in PO or PTAS.

- Note that neither definition preserves membership in PO.

We can now define the notion of complete problems for the classes APX, log-APX and poly-APX.

Definition 2.45 [APX-completeness]   *An* NPO *problem* Π *is APX-hard if every APX problem is AP-reducible to* Π. *If, in addition,* Π *is in APX, then* Π *is APX-complete.*

Example 2.46 MAX CUT *is APX-complete* [52].

Definition 2.47 [log-APX and poly-APX-completeness]   *An* NPO *problem* Π *is* log-APX-hard   (poly-APX-hard) *if every* log-APX (poly-APX) *problem is A-reducible to* Π. *If, in addition,* Π *is in* log-APX (poly-APX)*, then* Π *is* log-APX-complete (poly-APX-complete).

Example 2.48 MIN SET COVER *is* log-APX-*complete and* MAX CLIQUE *is* poly-APX-*complete.*

Chapter 3

Boolean Constraint Satisfaction Problems

We introduce Boolean constraint satisfaction problems in this chapter. We define several classes of constraint satisfaction problems, corresponding to the different classes NP, PSPACE, NC, #P, and NPO. The unifying concept behind all the classes, and all problems within a class, is the presentation of the input instances. An instance of any problem in any one of the classes has the same canonical form: it is always presented as m constraints over n Boolean variables! The difference in the classes comes up from the difference in the goals. For example, in the NP version of the problem, the goal is to find an assignment that satisfies all the given constraints; while in one of the NPO versions, the goal is to find an assignment that satisfies the maximum number of constraints.

Within any given class, there are infinitely many problems. The problems differ in the nature of constraints that are allowed. For example, in the NP version of constraint satisfaction, two of the problems are (1) 3-SAT and (2) satisfiability of linear equations modulo two. The difference between the two problems is the nature of the underlying constraints. In order to be able to specify a computational problem in terms of its underlying constraint structure, one needs a finite specification of the set of constraints. In order to achieve this objective, we distinguish *constraints* from their *applications*. For example, there are $\Omega(n^3)$ different clauses of length 3, when applied to n Boolean variables. However it is clear that the underlying template only needs to include all the different constraints on up to 3 variables; and the rest can be achieved by specifying to which (ordered) subset of variables is a basic constraint being applied. Since there are only finitely many (an easy count leads to an upper bound of 26) different clauses on three specified variables, it becomes clear that the constraints of 3-SAT can be finitely specified. (In our final specification, we will do so with four constraints.) This distinction between constraints and their applications is formalized next. Once we formalize this distinction, we present the different classes of constraint satisfaction problems that we will study. We also present examples of some representative problems arising in these classes.

3.1   Constraints and constraint applications

We start with the formal definition of a constraint. Throughout this work, a constraint is simply a Boolean function on a finite Boolean domain, given by some canonical description, such as a truth table.

Definition 3.1 [constraint] *A constraint is a Boolean function* $f : \{0,1\}^k \to \{0,1\}$, *where* k *is a non-negative integer called the* arity *of* f. *We say that* f *is* satisfied *by an assignment* $s \in \{0,1\}^k$ *if* $f(s) = 1$. *A constraint with no satisfying assignments is called* unsatisfiable.

Example 3.2 *Some frequently used constraint functions are as follows:*

- *Unary functions:* $\mathsf{F}(x) = \bar{x}$, $\mathsf{T}(x) = x$.

- *Binary functions:* $\mathsf{OR}_0(x,y) = x \vee y$, $\mathsf{OR}_1(x,y) = \bar{x} \vee y$, $\mathsf{OR}_2(x,y) = \bar{x} \vee \bar{y}$, $\mathsf{XOR}(x,y) = (x \wedge \bar{y}) \vee (\bar{x} \wedge y)$, $\mathsf{REP}(x,y) = (x \wedge y) \vee (\bar{x} \wedge \bar{y})$.

- *Ternary function:* $\mathsf{One\_in\_Three}(x,y,z) = (x \vee y \vee z) \wedge (\bar{x} \vee \bar{y}) \wedge (\bar{x} \vee \bar{z}) \wedge (\bar{y} \vee \bar{z})$.

- *Other functions:*

  - *The OR functions:* $\mathsf{OR}_{k,j}(x_1,\dots,x_k) = \bar{x}_1 \vee \cdots \vee \bar{x}_j \vee x_{j+1} \vee \cdots \vee x_k$. *Note that if* $k = 2$, *we simply omit* k, *getting* $\mathsf{OR}_j = \mathsf{OR}_{2,j}$.
  - *The XOR functions:* $\mathsf{XOR}_p(x_1,\dots,x_p) = x_1 \oplus \cdots \oplus x_p$ *and* $\mathsf{XNOR}_p(x_1,\dots,x_p) = \neg(x_1 \oplus \cdots \oplus x_p)$, *for* $p \geq 3$.

The next definition describes how constraints may be applied to a large number of variables. Notice that the fact that the representation of the domain was not very significant to the notion of a *constraint*. However a careful parsing of the following definition, will reveal that the representation of variables does become relevant to the notion of a constraint application.

Definition 3.3 [constraint application] *Given* n *Boolean variables* $x_1,\dots,x_n$, *a constraint* f *of arity* k, *and indices* $i_1,\dots,i_k \in \{1,\dots,n\}$, *the pair* $\langle f, (i_1,\dots,i_k) \rangle$ *is referred to as an* application *of the constraint* f *to* $x_1,\dots,x_n$. *An assignment* $x_i = s_i$ *for* $i \in \{1,\dots,n\}$ *and* $s_i \in \{0,1\}$, *satisfies* the application *if* $f(s_{i_1},\dots,s_{i_k}) = 1$. *In the interest of readability, we will often denote a constraint application* $\langle f,(i_1,\dots,i_k)\rangle$ *by* $f(x_{i_1},\dots,x_{i_k})$.

Definition 3.4 [constraint set] *A constraint set* $\mathcal{F} = \{f_1,\dots,f_l\}$ *is a finite collection of satisfiable constraints.*

We also refer to a constraint set as a *constraint family*.

It is without any loss of generality that we restrict our attention to satisfiable constraints — presence of constraint functions that can never be satisfied does not alter the tractability of any of the problems studied here.

Definition 3.5 [$\mathcal{F}$-collection of constraints] *A collection of constraint applications of the form* $\{\langle f_j,(i_1(j),\dots,i_{k_j}(j))\rangle\}_{j=1}^{m}$ *for some positive integer* m, *on Boolean variables* $x_1,x_2,\dots,x_n$, *where* $f_j \in \mathcal{F}$ *and* k_j *is the arity of* f_j, *is referred to as an* $\mathcal{F}$-collection of constraints.

We say that an assignment satisfies an $\mathcal{F}$-collection of constraints if it satisfies every constraint in the collection.

3.2 Constraint satisfaction problems

We now define the classes of problems that we study. A problem in each of these classes is characterized by a constraint set $\mathcal{F}$ which determines the nature of constraints that are allowed in the input instance to the problem. The input to any problem in each class is identical, namely, an $\mathcal{F}$-collection of constraints, and it is only the goal that varies across the various classes.

3.2.1 Decision and counting problems

We start by defining the constraint satisfaction version of the class NP.

Definition 3.6 [satisfiability problem (SAT($\mathcal{F}$))] *The satisfiability problem* SAT($\mathcal{F}$) *is to decide whether there exists an assignment that satisfies a given $\mathcal{F}$-collection of constraints.*

Example 3.7 *The classical 2-SAT problem is the same as* SAT($\{OR_0, OR_1, OR_2\}$), *while the 3-SAT problem is the same as* SAT($\{OR_{3,0}, OR_{3,1}, OR_{3,2}, OR_{3,3}\}$).

In a manner analogous to how we derived the definition of class #P from the class NP, we may also define the counting version of constraint satisfaction problems.

Definition 3.8 [satisfiability counting problem (#SAT($\mathcal{F}$))] *The satisfiability counting problem* #SAT($\mathcal{F}$) *is to find the number of distinct assignments that satisfy a given $\mathcal{F}$-collection of constraints.*

We will also study the problem of evaluating a quantified collection of constraints. A *quantified $\mathcal{F}$-expression* is an expression of the form $\mathcal{Q}_1 x_1 \ldots \mathcal{Q}_n x_n \mathcal{C}$, where $\mathcal{C}$ is an $\mathcal{F}$-collection of constraints over the set of variables $\{x_1, \ldots, x_n\}$ and $\mathcal{Q}_i$ is either the quantifier "for all" or "exists", for $i = 1, \ldots, n$.

Definition 3.9 [quantified satisfiability problem (QSAT($\mathcal{F}$))] *The quantified satisfiability problem* QSAT($\mathcal{F}$) *is to decide whether a given quantified $\mathcal{F}$-expression is true.*

Quantified satisfiability problems form a natural subclass of PSPACE problems; and include some PSPACE-complete problems. Classification of the complexity of every problem in SAT($\mathcal{F}$), #SAT($\mathcal{F}$) and QSAT($\mathcal{F}$) will be carried out in Chapter 6.

3.2.2 Optimization problems

In contrast to the decision and counting worlds, where there is essentially a unique way to obtain constraint satisfaction versions of the corresponding class, the case of optimization is somewhat more general. Here we end up with four different classes!

Recall that a generic NPO problem is specified by a four-tuple $(\mathcal{I}, S, m, \text{OPT})$, where $\mathcal{I}$ describes the space of instances, S describes the space of feasible solutions, m defines the value of a given solution and OPT prescribes the goal (max or min). In all the problems we consider, the instances ($\mathcal{I}$) are still the same: $\mathcal{F}$-collections of constraints. The four classes are defined by two attributes. The first attribute is simply by the OPT parameter. Two classes have this set to max, while two other classes below set this to min. The other attribute distinguishing the four classes below is their definition of feasible solutions (S) and the manner in which the value of a feasible solution is determined (m).

The first two classes below treat all solutions as feasible. Thus $S(x) = \{0,1\}^n$ for all instances on n variables. The $\mathcal{F}$-collection of constraints work their way into the value of a solution — the solutions that satisfy more constraints are better. Thus, in the first class below, the objective is to maximize the number of satisfied constraints while in the second class below the objective is to minimize the number of unsatisfied constraints.

Definition 3.10 [MAX constraint satisfaction problem (MAX SAT($\mathcal{F}$))]   *The* MAX *constraint satisfaction problem* MAX SAT($\mathcal{F}$) *is to find an assignment that satisfies a maximum number of constraints in a given $\mathcal{F}$-collection of constraints.*

Example 3.11 *The problem* MAX CUT *can be expressed as* MAX SAT($\{$XOR$\}$).

Definition 3.12 [MIN constraint satisfaction problem (MIN SAT($\mathcal{F}$))]   *The* MIN *constraint satisfaction problem* MIN SAT($\mathcal{F}$) *is to find an assignment that minimizes the number of unsatisfied constraints in a given $\mathcal{F}$-collection of constraints.*

Example 3.13 *The problem* s,t-MIN CUT *can be expressed as* MIN SAT($\{$F, T, OR$_1\}$).

In the next two classes, we revert to the notion that constraints need to be enforced. Thus an instance, i.e., an $\mathcal{F}$-collection of constraints, has as its feasible solution space, the assignments that satisfy the collection. The objective function in these problems is then set to a simple one, that of maximizing (or minimizing) the sum of the variables (or equivalently the number of variables set to 1).

Definition 3.14 [MAX ones problem (MAX ONES($\mathcal{F}$))]   *The* MAX *Ones problem* MAX ONES($\mathcal{F}$) *is to find an assignment that satisfies all constraints in a given $\mathcal{F}$-collection of constraints and maximizes the number of variables that are set to true.*

Example 3.15 *The problem* MAX CLIQUE *can be expressed as* MAX ONES($\{$OR$_2\}$).

Definition 3.16 [MIN ones problem (MIN ONES($\mathcal{F}$))]   *The* MIN *Ones problem* MIN ONES($\mathcal{F}$) *is to find an assignment that satisfies all constraints in a given $\mathcal{F}$-collection of constraints and minimizes the number of variables that are set to true.*

Example 3.17 *The problem* MIN VERTEX COVER *can be expressed as* MIN ONES($\{$OR$_0\}$).

Together, these classes describe a rich variety of optimization problems and this is further discussed in Chapter 7.

In the study of optimization problems, it is natural to consider weighted problems. Constraint satisfaction problems generalize naturally to include this aspect, once we introduce notions of weighted constraints and weighted variables.

Definition 3.18 [constraint/variable weighted $\mathcal{F}$-collection of constraints]   *An $\mathcal{F}$-collection of constraints with m constraint applications on n variables is called a* constraint weighted $\mathcal{F}$-collection of constraints *if we are given m non-negative integers $w_1, \ldots, w_m$ such that w_j denotes the weight of the jth constraint application. The $\mathcal{F}$-collection of constraints is called a* variable weighted $\mathcal{F}$-collection of constraints *if we are given n non-negative integers $w_1, \ldots, w_n$ such that w_i denotes the weight of the ith variable.*

Given a subset S of weighted constraint applications, we let the weight of S be the sum of weight of the constraints in S. We now define the weighted version of MAX SAT.

Definition 3.19 [weighted MAX constraint satisfaction problem (Weighted MAX SAT($\mathcal{F}$))]
The weighted MAX constraint satisfaction problem Weighted MAX SAT($\mathcal{F}$) *is to find an assignment that maximizes the weight of the satisfied constraints in a given constraint weighted $\mathcal{F}$-collection of constraints.*

We can define *weighted* MIN *constraint satisfaction problem,* referred to as Weighted MIN SAT($\mathcal{F}$), in an analogous manner.

In a variable weighted $\mathcal{F}$-collection of constraints, for an assignment to the variables, we let the weight of the assignment be the sum of weight of the variables set to 1 by the assignment.

Definition 3.20 [weighted MAX ones problem (Weighted MAX ONES($\mathcal{F}$))] *The* weighted MAX ones problem Weighted MAX ONES($\mathcal{F}$) *is to find a satisfying assignment of maximum weight for a given variable weighted $\mathcal{F}$-collection of constraints.*

Similarly, the *weighted* MIN *ones problem* Weighted MIN ONES($\mathcal{F}$) is to find a satisfying assignment of minimum weight for a given variable weighted $\mathcal{F}$-collection of constraints. Chapter 7 classifies the approximability of every (weighted and unweighted) optimization problem described above.

Chapter 4

Characterizations of Constraint Functions

In this chapter we study some basic properties of Boolean functions. To motivate this study, recall that in future chapters we intend to classify the complexity of all problems within a class, say, all problems of the form $\mathsf{SAT}(\mathcal{F})$. We have also indicated that all problems within a class will fall into one of finitely many equivalence subclasses. For instance, we will later show that every $\mathsf{SAT}(\mathcal{F})$ problem is either in P or is NP-complete. Further, for each such classification result, we will present a finite description of rules that can be applied to determine which equivalence class a given family $\mathcal{F}$ falls in. To prepare for such finite descriptions, in this chapter we describe and study some basic properties of Boolean functions. In later chapters we will then use these properties to explain results such as when a given family $\mathcal{F}$ is such that $\mathsf{SAT}(\mathcal{F})$ is NP-complete, and when it is in P.

In addition to describing the properties, we also give some characterizations of functions that satisfy (or do not satisfy) a given property. As an example, consider constraints that can be described by linear constraints over the finite field of two elements. When a family of functions $\mathcal{F}$ possesses this property, then we will show that $\mathsf{SAT}(\mathcal{F})$ is in P. On the other hand, when a family of functions does not possess this property, then $\mathsf{SAT}(\mathcal{F})$ may be intractable. However to show the latter result, we need a constructive way of exploiting the fact that $\mathcal{F}$ is *not* given by linear constraints. Lemma 4.10 describes a "witness" to the property of not being a linear functions. In later chapters this property will be crucial in establishing hardness results for non-linear families of functions. We provide such characterizations for numerous properties of functions.

4.1 Notation

We will frequently use the following four Boolean operations on assignments:

- $\bar{s} = \vec{1} - s$ is defined by $\bar{s}(x) = 1$ iff $s(x) = 0$ and $\bar{s}(x) = 0$ otherwise,

- $s = s_1 \oplus s_2$ is defined by $s(x) = 1$ iff $s_1(x) \neq s_2(x)$ and $s(x) = 0$ otherwise,

- $s = s_1 \cap s_2$ is defined by $s(x) = 1$ iff $s_1(x) = s_2(x) = 1$ and $s(x) = 0$ otherwise,

25

- $s = s_1 \cup s_2$ is defined by $s(x) = 0$ if and only if $s_1(x) = s_2(x) = 0$ and $s(x) = 1$ otherwise, and

- $s = \text{MAJORITY}(s_1, s_2, s_3) = (s_1 \cup s_2) \cap (s_2 \cup s_3) \cap (s_3 \cup s_1)$.

Given an assignment s to an underlying set of variables, $Z(s)$ and $O(s)$ denote the set of positions corresponding to variables set to zero and one, respectively. In other words, given an assignment $s = s_1 s_2 \ldots s_n$ to $x_1, x_2, \ldots, x_n$, where $s_i \in \{0, 1\}$, we have $Z(s) = \{i \mid s_i = 0\}$ and $O(s) = \{i \mid s_i = 1\}$. We denote by $s[1 \to *]$ the set of $2^{|O(s)|}$ assignments which agree with s on positions in $Z(s)$ and take all possible values on the remaining variables; we define the set $s[0 \to *]$ in an analogous manner.

4.2 Representations of constraint functions

A Boolean function f may be expressed in a number of logically equivalent representations. There are two particular logical representations that we will use extensively through out this work. These representations are defined in terms of *minterms* and *maxterms*.

Definition 4.1 [minterm] *Given a function* $f(x_1, x_2, \ldots, x_k)$, *a subset of literals defined over the variables* x_i's *is called a* minterm *if setting each literal to true forces the function to be satisfied, and if it is a minimal such collection.*

We express a minterm $m = \{l_1, l_2, \ldots, l_M\}$, where each l_j is x_i or $\bar{x}_i$ for some x_i, as $\bigwedge_{j=1}^{M} l_j$. Thus if $m_1, m_2, \ldots, m_p$ are all the minterms of a function f then f may be represented as $\bigvee_{i=1}^{p} m_i$. This is referred to as the *minterm representation* of a function f.

Definition 4.2 [maxterm] *Given a function* $f(x_1, x_2, \ldots, x_k)$, *a subset of literals defined over the variables* x_i's *is called a* maxterm *if setting each of the literals false determines the function to be false, and if it is a minimal such collection.*

We express a maxterm $m = \{l_1, l_2, \ldots, l_M\}$, where each l_j is x_i or $\bar{x}_i$ for some x_i, as $\bigvee_{j=1}^{M} l_j$. Thus if $m_1, m_2, \ldots, m_q$ are all the maxterms of a function f, then f may be represented as $\bigwedge_{i=1}^{q} m_i$. This is referred to as the *maxterm representation* of a function f.

Example 4.3 *The minterm representation of the function* $\text{XOR}(x, y)$ *is* $(x \wedge \bar{y}) \vee (\bar{x} \wedge y)$ *while its maxterm representation is* $(x \vee y) \wedge (\bar{x} \vee \bar{y})$.

Notice that the minterm (maxterm) representation is a special case of the Disjunctive Normal Form (DNF) (Conjunctive Normal Form (CNF)) representation of a function.

A function may have several DNF (CNF) representations; but the minterm (maxterm) representation is unique by definition.

4.3 Properties of constraint functions

We now define certain properties of constraint functions that arise frequently in our study.

Definition 4.4 *A constraint f is said to be*

0-valid *if* $f(0, \ldots, 0) = 1$.

1-valid *if* $f(1, \ldots, 1) = 1$.

weakly positive (weakly negative) *if f is expressible as a CNF-formula having at most one negated (unnegated[4]) variable in each clause.*

bijunctive *if f is expressible as a 2CNF-formula.*

affine *if f is expressible as a system of linear equations over* $\mathrm{GF}(2)$*; that is, it is equivalent to a system of linear equations of the forms $v_1 \oplus \cdots \oplus v_n = 0$ and $v_1 \oplus \cdots \oplus v_n = 1$, where $\oplus$ denotes the exclusive or connective.*

affine with width 2 *if f is expressible as a system of linear equations over $GF(2)$ with at most two variables per equation.*

2-monotone *if f is expressible as a DNF-formula either of the form $(x_1 \wedge \cdots \wedge x_p)$ or $(\bar{y}_1 \wedge \cdots \wedge \bar{y}_q)$ or $(x_1 \wedge \cdots \wedge x_p) \vee (\bar{y}_1 \wedge \cdots \wedge \bar{y}_q)$.*

IHS-B+ *(for* Implicative Hitting Set-Bounded+) *if it is expressible as a CNF formula where the clauses are of one of the following types: $\bar{x}_1$, or $\bar{x}_1 \vee x_2$, or $x_1 \vee \cdots \vee x_k$ for some positive integer k.*

IHS-B− *if it is expressible as a CNF formula where the clauses are of one of the following types: x_1, or $\bar{x}_1 \vee x_2$, or $\bar{x}_1 \vee \cdots \vee \bar{x}_k$ for some positive integer k.*

C-closed *if for all assignments s, $f(s) = f(\bar{s})$.*

The above definitions also generalize to sets (families) of constraints. For instance, a constraint family $\mathcal{F}$ is called an *affine family* if every constraint in $\mathcal{F}$ is affine. Additionally, we refer to a constraint set $\mathcal{F}$ as a *Horn family* if $\mathcal{F}$ is either weakly positive or weakly negative, and as a *IHS-B family* if the family is either a IHS-B+ family or a IHS-B− family.

We stress that the properties listed above do not partition the Boolean functions. (In fact, the function One_in_Three (which is satisfied when exactly one of its three arguments is 1) does not possess any of the properties listed above; while the function REP possesses all the properties listed above!) However these properties play a central role in determining when a given computational task is easy, versus when it is hard. For example, Schaefer's theorem (to be proved later) will show that a SAT($\mathcal{F}$) problem is in P if and only if $\mathcal{F}$ is 0-valid or 1-valid or bijunctive or affine or a Horn family. Classification results for other classes described earlier will assume a similar flavor.

4.4 Characterization lemmas

In this section we develop some characterizations of the properties described above. The natural definitions of the properties, as given earlier, make it easy to establish that a function has a given property. The characterizations that we now develop help us identify witnesses to the fact that a function does not satisfy a given property. We start by proving some simple closure properties.

---

[4]Such clauses are usually called Horn clauses.

Lemma 4.5 *Let f be a weakly positive (weakly negative/ bijunctive/ IHS-B+/ IHS-B−) constraint. Then any constraint f' derived from f by setting some subset of its variables to constants (0/1) and existentially quantifying over some subset of remaining variables is also weakly positive (weakly negative / bijunctive / IHS-B+ / IHS-B−).*

Proof: It is easy to see that a function f remains weakly positive (weakly negative / affine/ affine with width 2/ bijunctive/ IHS-B+ / IHS-B−) when any subset of variables is restricted to a constant. Thus we only need to consider the case when a subset of variables is existentially quantified. Using a straightforward inductive argument, it suffices to consider quantification over a single variable, say, y. In what follows, we assume that we are given the function as a CNF expression

$$f(x_1,\ldots,x_k,y) = \left(\bigwedge_{j_0 \in X_0}(C_{j_0}^0(\vec{x}) \vee y)\right) \bigwedge \left(\bigwedge_{j_1 \in X_1}(C_{j_1}^1(\vec{x}) \vee \bar{y})\right) \bigwedge \left(\bigwedge_{j \in X} C_j(\vec{x})\right)$$

where X_0, X_1 and X_2 are the indices of the clauses in which y appears as a positive literal, negative literal, and does not appear, respectively. Moreover, the clauses $C_{j_0}^0$, $C_{j_1}^1$ and C_j involve only literals on the variables $x_1,\ldots,x_k$. We assume that each clause in the above representation satisfies the property of its underlying function. Now consider the function

$$f'(x_1,\ldots,x_k) \overset{\text{def}}{=} \exists y\ f(x_1,\ldots,x_k,y).$$

We first show a simple transformation which creates a CNF expression for f'. Define $|X_0| \times |X_1|$ clauses $C_{j_0 j_1}'(\vec{x}) \overset{\text{def}}{=} C_{j_0}^0(\vec{x}) \bigvee C_{j_1}^1(\vec{x})$ with $j_0 \in X_0$ and $j_1 \in X_1$. We now show that for every $\vec{x}$,

$$f'(\vec{x}) = \left(\bigwedge_{j_0 \in X_0} \bigwedge_{j_1 \in X_1} C_{j_0 j_1}'(\vec{x})\right) \bigwedge \left(\bigwedge_{j \in X} C_j(\vec{x})\right). \tag{4.1}$$

Suppose $f'(\vec{x}) = 1$. In this case there must exist a y such that $f(\vec{x}, y) = 1$, and hence an $\vec{x}$ such that all the clauses $C_j(\vec{x})$ as well as all the clauses $C_{j_y}^y(\vec{x})$ are satisfied. Thus the right hand side expression above is satisfied. Conversely, if the right hand side expression above is satisfied then we claim that $\vec{x}$ must satisfy either all the clauses C^0 or all the clauses C^1. Assume, by way of contradiction, that the clauses $C_{j_0}^0$ and $C_{j_1}^1$ are not satisfied. Then the clause $C_{j_0 j_1}'$ is not satisfied either. A contradiction. Thus by setting $y = i$ such that all clauses C^i are satisfied, we find that $f(\vec{x}, y)$ is satisfied. This in turn implies that $f'(\vec{x}) = 1$.

To conclude the proof, we need to verify that f', as defined by the right hand side of (4.1), satisfies the same properties as f. We only need to consider clauses of the form $C_{j_0 j_1}'(\vec{x})$ since all other clauses are directly from the expression for f. We verify below for the various properties.

weakly positive/weakly negative: If f is weakly positive, then the clause $C_{j_0}^0$ involves at most one negated variable, and the clause $C_{j_1}^1$ involves no negated variable. Thus the clause defining $C_{j_0 j_1}^{01}$ also has at most one negated variable. A similar analysis applies if f is weakly negative.

bijunctive: If f is 2CNF, then the clauses $C_{j_0}^0$ and $C_{j_1}^1$ are of length 1 and hence the clause $C_{j_0 j_1}'$ is of length at most 2.

IHS-B+ / IHS-B−: If f is IHS-B+, then the clause $C_{j_0}^0$ has either has only one literal which is negated or has only positive literals. Furthermore, $C_{j_1}^1$ has at most one positive literal. Thus $C'_{j_0 j_1}$ either has only positive literals or has at most two literals one of which is negated. Hence $C'_{j_0 j_1}$ is also IHS-B+. Similarly if f in IHS-B−, then the clause $C'_{j_0 j_1}$ is also IHS-B−. □

Lemma 4.6 *Let f be an affine (affine width 2) constraint. Then any constraint f' derived from f by setting some subset of its variables to constants $(0/1)$ and existentially quantifying over a subset of the remaining variables, is also affine (affine width 2).*

Proof: The proof of this lemma is similar to Lemma 4.5, except that we represent the function as a conjunction of basic affine functions rather than as a conjunction of clauses. We omit the details as a simple exercise to the reader. □

The closure property described in Lemma 4.5 allows us to prove the following central fact about the maxterms of weakly positive (weakly negative / bijunctive / IHS-B+/ IHS-B−) functions.

Lemma 4.7 *A constraint f is weakly positive (weakly negative / bijunctive / IHS-B+/ IHS-B−) constraint if and only if all its maxterms are weakly positive (weakly negative / bijunctive / IHS-B+/ IHS-B−).*

Proof The proof technique is once again common to all the properties. We focus on the weakly positive case and towards the end, sketch the modifications needed for other properties.

Using the maxterm representation of f, it is clear that if all maxterms are weakly positive, then f is weakly positive We now consider the converse. Suppose f has a (non-weakly-positive) maxterm of the form:

$$\bar{x}_1 \vee \bar{x}_2 \cdots \vee \bar{x}_p \vee x_{p+1} \vee \cdots \vee x_{p+q},$$

where $p \geq 2$ and $q \geq 0$. Consider the function

$$f'(x_1, x_2) = \exists x_{p+q+1}, \ldots, x_k f(x_1, x_2, 1^{p-2}0^q, x_{p+q+1}, \ldots, x_k).$$

By definition of a maxterm, any assignment setting $x_1 = \cdots = x_p = 1$ and $x_{p+1} = \cdots x_q = 0$ leaves f unsatisfied. Thus $f'(11) = 0$. Further, the minimality of this maxterm implies that there exist assignments of the form $s_1 = 01^{p-1}0^q a_{p+q+1} \ldots a_k$ and $s_2 = 101^{p-2}0^q b_{p+q+1} \ldots b_k$ such that $f(s_1) = f(s_2) = 1$. Hence we get $f'(01) = f'(10) = 1$. Now depending on the value of $f'(00)$, we find that $f'(x_1 x_2)$ is either the function $x_1 \oplus x_2$ or $\bar{x}_1 \vee \bar{x}_2$, neither of which is weakly positive. By Lemma 4.5, this implies f is not weakly positive.

An identical analysis applies for the case of weakly negative constraints. For the case of bijunctive constraints, a similar analysis gives a ternary function f' which is not bijunctive if some maxterm of f were not bijunctive. Finally, if some maxterm of f were weakly positive (weakly negative) but not IHS-B+ (IHS-B−), we get a ternary function f' that is not monotone positive (negative). In each case, we can apply Lemma 4.5 to get the desired result. □

We are now ready to develop characterizations that are specific to the properties described in the previous section. We start with the Horn families.

Lemma 4.8 [40] *A function f is a weakly positive (weakly negative) function if and only if for all assignments s_1, s_2 that satisfy f the assignment $s_1 \cup s_2$ ($s_1 \cap s_2$) is also satisfying.*

Proof: In one direction it suffices to verify that if s_1 and s_2 satisfy a weakly positive function of the form $\bar{x}_1 \vee x_2 \vee \cdots x_k$ (i.e., a single clause), then so does $s_1 \cup s_2$ and this is easily verified. By arguing so for every maxterm of a function f we get one direction, namely, if f is weakly positive then for any two satisfying assignments s_1, s_2, $s_1 \cup s_2$ also satisfies f.

For the other direction, let f be a function that is not weakly positive. By Lemma 4.7 we know that f has a non-weakly-positive maxterm. Say the maxterm is $\bar{x}_1 \vee \bar{x}_2 \cdots \vee \bar{x}_p \vee x_{p+1} \vee \cdots \vee x_{p+q}$, where $p \geq 2$ and $q \geq 0$. Maximality implies there exist assignments of the form $s_1 = 01^{p-1}0^q a_{p+q+1} \ldots a_k$ and $s_2 = 101^{p-2}0^q b_{p+q+1} \ldots b_k$ such that $f(s_1) = f(s_2) = 1$. But $s_1 \cup s_2$ is of the form $0^p 1^q c_{p+q+1} \ldots c_k$ and cannot satisfy f: this is a contradiction. $\square$

Lemma 4.9 [bijunctive characterization] [82] *A function f is a bijunctive function if and only if for all assignments s_1, s_2, s_3 that satisfy f, the assignment $\mathrm{MAJORITY}(s_1, s_2, s_3)$ is also satisfying.*

Proof: The proof of this lemma is very similar to the proof of Lemma 4.8 above and hence omitted. $\square$

Lemma 4.10 [affine characterization] [82, 19] *A function f is affine if and only if for all satisfying assignments s_1, s_2, s_3, the assignment $s_1 \oplus s_2 \oplus s_3$ is also satisfying. Alternatively, the function f is affine if and only if for any fixed satisfying assignment s_0, the assignment $s_1 \oplus s_2 \oplus s_0$, where s_1, s_2 are any two satisfying assignments, is also satisfying.*

Proof: The first characterization above follows from a classical and well-known characterization of affine subspaces in linear algebra. For completeness, we go through the basic steps here. To see the forward direction, note that it suffices to verify the assertion for the basic affine functions XOR_p and XNOR_p, since other affine functions are just conjunctions of such functions. It is straightforward to verify that if s_1, s_2 and s_3 are p-ary strings with odd number of 1's (and thus satisfying XOR_p), then $s_1 \oplus s_2 \oplus s_3$ also has an odd number of ones. This is similarly true for XNOR_p.

To see the converse of the first characterization, we assume f is a k-ary predicate that satisfies the condition that if s_1, s_2 and s_3 satisfy f, then so does $s_1 \oplus s_2 \oplus s_3$. We will show that this implies f is affine. Let $\vec{x} = \langle x_1, \ldots, x_k \rangle$ and $\vec{x}' = \langle x_2, \ldots, x_k \rangle$. Let $f_0(\vec{x}') = f(0, \vec{x}')$ and $f_1(\vec{x}') = f(1, \vec{x}')$. The function f_0 (resp., f_1) satisfies the property that if s_1', s_2' and s_3' satisfy f_0 (resp., f_1), then so does $s_1' \oplus s_2' \oplus s_3'$. Thus, by induction on k, we have that both f_0 and f_1 are affine. Now if f_0 doesn't have any satisfying assignments, then $f(\vec{x}) = (x_1 = 1) \wedge f_1(\vec{x}')$ and thus f is affine. A similar argument applies to f_1. So assume both f_0 and f_1 have satisfying assignments, say s_1' and s_2', respectively. Let $s_1 = 0s_1'$ and $s_2 = 1s_2'$. Taking any string $s_3 = 1s'$ and using the fact that $s_1 \oplus s_2 \oplus s_3$ satisfies f if and only if s_3 does, we get $f_1(s') = f_0(s_1' \oplus s_2' \oplus s')$. Let A' be a matrix and $\vec{b}'$ be a vector such that $f_0(\vec{x}') = 1$ if and only if $A'\vec{x}' = b'$. (Such a pair exists since f_0 is affine.) Then, using the fact that $f_1(s') = f_0(s_1' \oplus s_2' \oplus s')$, we get $f_1(\vec{x}') = 1$ if and only if $A'(\vec{x}' \oplus s_1' \oplus s_2') = \vec{b}'$. Let $A = [A'(s_1' \oplus s_2')|A']$, i.e., A is the matrix A' with one additional column $A'(s_1' \oplus s_2')$ added in from the left. Then, we have $A\vec{x} = \vec{b}'$ if and only if $f(\vec{x}) = 1$ and thus f is also affine. This completes the proof of the first characterization.

To see the second characterization above, let us fix a satisfying assignment s_0 for f. If f is affine, then using the first characterization above, we know that for all assignments s_1, s_2

that satisfy f, $s_1 \oplus s_2 \oplus s_0$ also satisfies f. Conversely, suppose that for all assignments s_1, s_2 that satisfy f, the assignment $s_1 \oplus s_2 \oplus s_0$ is also satisfying. Let s_3 be any assignment that satisfies f. By assumption $(s_1 \oplus s_2 \oplus s_0) \oplus s_3 \oplus s_0$ satisfies f. But, $(s_1 \oplus s_2 \oplus s_0) \oplus s_3 \oplus s_0 = (s_1 \oplus s_2 \oplus s_3) \oplus (s_0 \oplus s_0) = s_1 \oplus s_2 \oplus s_3$, thus completing the proof. $\square$

Lemma 4.11 [affine with width-two characterization] *A function f is affine with width two if and only if it is affine and bijunctive.*

Proof: It is clear that if f is affine with width two, then it is affine and bijunctive. In particular, the constraint $x_i \oplus x_j$ can be expressed as the conjunction of $x_i \vee x_j$ and $\bar{x}_i \vee \bar{x}_j$; and the constraint $\bar{x}_i \oplus x_j$ can be expressed as the conjunction of $\bar{x}_i \vee x_j$ and $x_i \vee \bar{x}_j$.

To see the converse, let f be an affine and bijunctive function. Since f is bijunctive, all maxterms of f have at most two literals in them. The maxterms of size 1 are already affine constraints with width one; so we consider a maxterm of size 2. Suppose $x_1 \vee x_2$ is a maxterm. Then we claim $\bar{x}_1 \vee \bar{x}_2$ is also a maxterm. If not, then the function

$$g(x_1, x_2) \stackrel{\text{def}}{=} \exists x_3, \ldots, x_k \; f(x_1, \ldots, x_k)$$

equals the function $x_1 \vee x_2$ which is not affine, and this contradicts Lemma 4.6. But then we can replace the maxterms $x_1 \vee x_2$ and $\bar{x}_1 \vee \bar{x}_2$ by the constraint $x_1 \oplus x_2$ which is affine with width two. Proceeding like this for every maxterm, we obtain an affine representation of f with width two. $\square$

Definition 4.12 [0/1-consistent set] *A set $V \subseteq \{1, \ldots, k\}$ is 0-consistent (1-consistent) for a constraint $f : \{0,1\}^k \to \{0,1\}$ if and only if every assignment s with $Z(s) \supset V$ ($O(s) \supset V$) is a satisfying assignment for f.*

Lemma 4.13 [2-monotone-characterization] [54] *A function f is a 2-monotone function if and only if all the following conditions are satisfied:*

(a) for every satisfying assignment s of f, either $Z(s)$ is 0-consistent or $O(s)$ is 1-consistent.

(b) if V_1 is 1-consistent and V_2 is 1-consistent for f, then $V_1 \cap V_2$ is 1-consistent, and

(c) if V_1 is 0-consistent and V_2 is 0-consistent for f, then $V_1 \cap V_2$ is 0-consistent.

Proof: Suppose f is a 2-monotone function expressed as a sum of at most two terms satisfying the definition. Every satisfying assignment must satisfy one of the terms and this gives us property (a). Properties (b) and (c) are obtained from the fact that the function has at most one positive and one negative term.

Conversely, suppose the function f is not 2-monotone. We assume that we are given a minterm representation of f. Since f is not 2-monotone, it either has a minterm which is not monotone positive or monotone negative or it has more than one positive (or negative) minterm. In the former case, the function violates property (a), and in the latter case, it violates either property (b) or property (c). $\square$

The characterizations above conclude our first cut at understanding Boolean functions. In the next chapter we will set a more firm target on our exploration of Boolean functions. We will define a specific notion of how Boolean functions may "implement" other Boolean functions. The characterizations will turn out to be quite useful in establishing a wide variety of implementations.

Chapter 5

Implementation of Functions and Reductions

A complexity classification result for a class of problems is a statement describing a partial order among the problems in the class. As mentioned earlier, the central mechanism used in creating such a partial order is reduction, the process of transforming a given problem into another one. Since problems in our framework are specified via underlying constraint sets, the notion of a reduction between problems essentially corresponds to transformation between constraint sets. Toward this end, we now introduce a natural notion, called *implementation*, which is a mechanism for showing that the behavior of a given constraint can be "implemented" by some collection of functions. Just as the precise notion of reduction needed depends on the underlying class of problems, the specific notion of implementation needed varies with the underlying class of problems. In the remainder of this chapter, we formally introduce the notion of implementation and study its inherent connection to reductions. We then develop several results concerning the implementation power of various types of constraint families. A typical result here shows that all constraint families that lack a given property can implement some canonical function lacking the property. These results allow us to unify large classes of constraint families through a small number of canonical functions; this is a process central to our classification results.

5.1 Implementations

The following definition was explicitly formalized in [54] and its variants have been implicitly used by other researchers (see [19], for instance).

Definition 5.1 [α-implementation] *An $\mathcal{F}$-collection of constraint applications over a set of variables $\vec{x} = \{x_1, x_2, \ldots, x_p\}$ and $\vec{y} = \{y_1, y_2, \ldots, y_q\}$ is called an α-implementation of a Boolean function $f(\vec{x})$, where α is a positive integer, if and only if the following conditions are satisfied:*

(a) *no assignment of values to $\vec{x}$ and $\vec{y}$ can satisfy more than α constraints,*

(b) *for any assignment of values to $\vec{x}$ such that $f(\vec{x})$ is true, there exists an assignment of values to $\vec{y}$ such that precisely α constraints are satisfied,*

(c) *for any assignment of values to $\vec{x}$ such that $f(\vec{x})$ is false, no assignment of values to $\vec{y}$ can satisfy more than $(\alpha - 1)$ constraints.*

We refer to the set $\vec{x}$ as the function variables *and the set $\vec{y}$ as the* auxiliary variables.

We will say that $\mathcal{F}$ *implements* a function f if there is an $\mathcal{F}$-collection of constraint applications that α_f-implements f for some constant α_f. Moreover, an implementation of a function f is called *strict* if for any assignment to $\vec{x}$ which does not satisfy f, there always exists an assignment to $\vec{y}$ such that precisely $(\alpha - 1)$ constraints are satisfied; an implementation is *perfect* if all constraints in the implementation are satisfiable whenever $f(\vec{x})$ evaluates to true and it is *faithful* if there is always a unique way of doing so. Thus a function f 1-implements itself strictly, perfectly and faithfully.

Example 5.2 *The family $\{\mathsf{OR}_0, \mathsf{F}\}$ strictly 3-implements the function $\mathsf{XOR}(x_1, x_2)$. Consider the constraint applications $\{(x_1 \vee x_2), (x_1 \vee x_2), \bar{x}_1, \bar{x}_2\}$. Then any assignment to x_1, x_2 that satisfies $\mathsf{XOR}(x_1, x_2)$ satisfies exactly 3 constraints in the above collection and, otherwise, exactly 2 constraints are satisfied. Thus this is a strict implementation. Notice that there are no auxiliary variables in this implementation.*

Example 5.3 *The family $\{\mathsf{XOR}\}$ strictly 2-implements the function $\mathsf{XNOR}(x_1, x_2)$ through the constraint applications $\{\mathsf{XOR}(x_1, y), \mathsf{XOR}(x_2, y)\}$. Moreover, this implementation is perfect and faithful. The variable y is an auxiliary variable.*

Example 5.4 *The family $\{\mathsf{OR}_0, \mathsf{F}\}$ strictly 6-implements the function $\mathsf{XNOR}(x_1, x_2)$ through the constraint applications $\{(x_1 \vee y), (x_1 \vee y), \bar{x}_1, \bar{y}, (x_2 \vee y), (x_2 \vee y), \bar{x}_2, \bar{y}\}$.*

Later we will show how Example 5.4 follows from Examples 5.2 and 5.3 by a general composition method. The following is an example of a perfect, but unfaithful, implementation.

Example 5.5 *The family $\{\mathsf{One\_in\_Three}, \mathsf{XOR}\}$ strictly and perfectly implements the function $\mathsf{OR}_{3,0}(x, y, z)$ through the constraint applications*

$$\left\{ \begin{array}{ccc} (x \oplus x'), & (y \oplus y'), & (z \oplus z'), \\ \mathsf{One\_in\_Three}(x', u_1, v_1), & \mathsf{One\_in\_Three}(y', u_2, v_2), & \mathsf{One\_in\_Three}(z', u_3, v_3), \\ & \mathsf{One\_in\_Three}(u_1, u_2, u_3) & \end{array} \right\}.$$

(Roughly, the first three constraints force x', y' and z' to be the negations of x, y and z. Thus if $x = y = z = 0$, then $x' = y' = z' = 1$, and thus all the u_i's and v_i's are forced to 0 by the first three $\mathsf{One\_in\_Three}$ constraints, but this does not allow the final constraint to be satisfied. It may be verified that if at least one of x, y or z is true, then there is a way to satisfy all constraints; further, in some cases there is more than one way to do so and hence the implementation is not faithful.)

In the next example we show that the function $\mathsf{One\_in\_Three}$ perfectly implements the function XOR. Intuitively, this should indicate that in the above implementation, the use of XOR could have replaced with the use of $\mathsf{One\_in\_Three}$. We will see later that this is indeed the case.

Example 5.6 *The family $\{\mathsf{One\_in\_Three}\}$ strictly, perfectly and faithfully implements the constraint $\mathsf{XOR}(x, y)$ through the constraint applications*

$$\{\mathsf{One\_in\_Three}(z_\mathsf{T}, z_\mathsf{F}, z_\mathsf{F}), \mathsf{One\_in\_Three}(x, y, z_\mathsf{F})\}.$$

Remark: The implementation above gives a nice example of how one may use "replication" of variables in constraint applications — notice the repeated occurrence of the variable z_F in the first application above. We will allow such replication throughout this monograph. However, this allowance is not necessary for most of the proofs. The proofs in, say, [56, 55] do not use the ability to replicate variables. This gives them a more refined look at some optimization problems; however, their proofs get significantly more cumbersome. We opt for more elegant proofs here.

Getting back to implementations, often we will be interested in families implementing other families. Specifically, we will focus much attention in showing that some family $\mathcal{F}_1$ implements every function in some other family $\mathcal{F}_2$.

Example 5.7 *The family* $\{OR_{3,0}, XOR\}$ *strictly, perfectly and faithfully implements every function in the family* $\{OR_{3,0}, OR_{3,1}, OR_{3,2}, OR_{3,3}\}$. *(For instance, the constraint* $OR_{3,2}(x, y, z)$ *is implemented by the constraints* $\{(x' \vee y' \vee z), (x' \oplus x), (y' \oplus y)\}$.*)*

The following lemma shows that the above described α-implementations of functions compose together.

Lemma 5.8 [composition lemma] [54] *If* $\mathcal{F}_f$ *can strictly (perfectly, faithfully) implement a function* f, *and* $\mathcal{F}_g$ *can strictly (perfectly, faithfully) implement a function* $g \in \mathcal{F}_f$, *then* $((\mathcal{F}_f \setminus \{g\}) \cup \mathcal{F}_g)$ *can strictly (perfectly, faithfully) implement the function* f.

Proof: Let $C_1, \ldots, C_p$ be constraint applications from $\mathcal{F}_f$ on variable set $\vec{x}, \vec{y}$ giving an α_f-implementation of f with $\vec{x}$ and $\vec{y}$ being the function and the auxiliary variables, respectively. Let $C'_1, \ldots, C'_q$ be constraint applications from $\mathcal{F}_g$ on variable set $\vec{x'}, \vec{z}$ yielding an α_g-implementation of g. Further let the first β constraints of $C_1, \ldots, C_p$ be applications of the constraint g.

We create a collection of $p + \beta(q-1)$ constraints from $(\mathcal{F}_f \setminus \{g\}) \cup \mathcal{F}_g$ on a set of variables $\vec{x}, \vec{y}, \vec{z}_1, \ldots, \vec{z}_\beta$ as follows. We include the constraint applications $C_{\beta+1}, \ldots, C_p$ on variables $\vec{x}, \vec{y}$ and for every constraint application C_j, for $j \in \{1, \ldots, \beta\}$, on variables $\vec{v}_j$ (a subset of variables from $\vec{x}, \vec{y}$), we place the constraints $C'_{1,j}, \ldots, C'_{q,j}$ on variable set $\vec{v}_j, \vec{z}_j$ with $\vec{z}_j$ being the auxiliary variables.

We now show that this collection of constraints is an α-implementation of f where $\alpha = \alpha_f + \beta(\alpha_g - 1)$. We start with properties (a) and (c).

Consider any assignment to $\vec{x}$ satisfying f. Then any assignment to $\vec{y}$ satisfies at most α_f constraints from the set $C_1, \ldots, C_p$. Let γ of these be from the set $C_1, \ldots, C_\beta$. Now for every $j \in \{1, \ldots, \beta\}$ any assignment to $\vec{z}_j$ satisfies at most α_g of the constraints $C'_{1,j}, \ldots, C'_{q,j}$. Furthermore, if the constraint C_j is not satisfied by the assignment to $\vec{x}, \vec{y}$, then at most $\alpha_g - 1$ constraints are satisfied. Thus the total number of constraints satisfied by any assignment is at most $\gamma(\alpha_g) + (\beta - \gamma)(\alpha_g - 1) + (\alpha_f - \gamma) = \alpha_f + \beta(\alpha_g - 1)$. This yields property (a) in Definition 5.1. Property (c) can be shown to hold in a similar manner.

We now show that if the implementations of f and g are strict (perfect, faithful), we also get property (b) and that the property of being strict (perfect, faithful) is preserved.

Let us first consider the case when both implementations are perfect (faithful). In this case for any assignment to $\vec{x}$ satisfying f, there exists an (a unique) assignment to $\vec{y}$ satisfying $C_1, \ldots, C_p$. Furthermore, for every $j \in \{1, \ldots, \beta\}$, there exists an (a unique) assignment to $\vec{z}_j$ satisfying all the constraints $C'_{1,j}, \ldots, C'_{q,j}$. Thus there exists an (a unique) assignment to $\vec{x}, \vec{y}, \vec{z'}_1, \ldots, \vec{z'}_\beta$ satisfying all $p + \beta(q - 1)$ constraints. This yields property (b) with perfectness (faithfulness).

We next consider the case when both implementations are strict. Given an assignment to $\vec{x}$ satisfying f there exists an assignment to $\vec{y}$ satisfying α_f constraints from $C_1, \ldots, C_p$. Say this assignment satisfies γ constraints from the set $C_1, \ldots, C_\beta$ and $\alpha_f - \gamma$ constraints from the set $C_{\beta+1}, \ldots, C_p$. Then for every $j \in \{1, \ldots, \beta\}$ such that the clause C_j is satisfied by this assignment to $\vec{x}, \vec{y}$, there exists an assignment to $\vec{z}_j$ satisfying α_g clauses from the set $C'_{1,j}, \ldots, C'_{q,j}$. Furthermore, for the remaining values of $j \in \{1, \ldots, \beta\}$, there exists an assignment to the variables $\vec{z}_j$ which satisfies $\alpha_g - 1$ of the constraints $C'_{1,j}, \ldots, C'_{q,j}$ (for the α_g-implementation is strict). This setting of $\vec{y}, \vec{z}_1, \ldots, \vec{z}_\beta$ satisfies $\gamma\alpha_g + (\beta-\gamma)(\alpha_g-1) + \alpha_f - \gamma = \alpha_f + \beta(\alpha_g - 1)$ of the m constraints. This yields property (b). It remains to be proved that in this case the implementation obtained by composition is strict. Given an assignment to $\vec{x}$ that does not satisfy f there exists an assignment to $\vec{y}$ satisfying $(\alpha_f - 1)$ constraints from $C_1, \ldots, C_p$ for the α_f-implementation is strict. Then, the same reasoning as above yields an assignment to $\vec{y}, \vec{z}_1, \ldots, \vec{z}_\beta$ that satisfies $\alpha_f + \beta(\alpha_g - 1) - 1$ of the constraints, thus proving the strictness of the implementation. □

Lemma 5.8 can be applied to Examples 5.5 and 5.6 to obtain the following example.

Example 5.9 *The family* {One_in_Three} *strictly and perfectly implements the function* $OR_{3,0}$. *(Set* $\mathcal{F}_f = \{XOR, One\_in\_Three\}$ *and* $\mathcal{F}_g = \{One\_in\_Three\}$ *and note that by Example 5.6, we have that* $\mathcal{F}_g$ *implements* XOR.*)*

Applying Lemma 5.8 several times, we get more interesting implementations, such as the following example.

Example 5.10 *The family* {One_in_Three} *strictly and perfectly implements every function in the family* $\{OR_{3,0}, OR_{3,1}, OR_{3,2}, OR_{3,3}\}$. *(Use the implementations of Examples 5.5, 5.6 and 5.7, and combine them all using Lemma 5.8.)*

Next we show a simple monotonicity property of implementations.

Lemma 5.11 *For integers* α, α' *with* $\alpha \leq \alpha'$, *if* $\mathcal{F}$ α-*implements* f *then* $\mathcal{F}$ α'-*implements* f. *Furthermore strictness and perfectness are preserved under this transformation.*

Proof: Let constraint applications $C_1, \ldots, C_m$ from $\mathcal{F}$ on $\vec{x}, \vec{y}$ form an α-implementation of f, and let $g \in \mathcal{F}$ be a constraint of arity k that is satisfiable. Also, let $C_{m+1}, \ldots, C_{m+\alpha'-\alpha}$ be $\alpha' - \alpha$ applications of the constraint g on new variables $z_1, \ldots, z_k$. Then the collection of constraints $C_1, \ldots, C_{m+\alpha'-\alpha}$ on variable set $\vec{x}, \vec{y}, \vec{z}$ form an α'-implementation of f. Furthermore, the transformation preserves strictness and perfectness. □

5.2   Reductions for classical problems

As might be already evident from the definition and properties of implementations, they provide us with a natural mechanism to do reductions between various satisfiability problems. A problem specified by a constraint set $\mathcal{F}_1$ can be reduced to one specified by another constraint set $\mathcal{F}_2$, if $\mathcal{F}_2$ can implement the constraint set $\mathcal{F}_1$ with appropriate properties. In this section we formalize this connection between implementations and reductions for decision, counting and quantified variants of the constraint satisfaction problems.

5.2.1 Decision problems

Since decision problems concern with the question of whether or not all constraint applications are satisfiable, the appropriate notion of implementations for reductions between decision problems is that of perfect implementation.

Lemma 5.12 *If* $\mathsf{SAT}(\mathcal{F})$ *is* NP-*hard and every constraint of* $\mathcal{F}$ *can be perfectly implemented by* $\mathcal{F}'$, *then* $\mathsf{SAT}(\mathcal{F}')$ *is also* NP-*hard.*

Proof: We prove that if every constraint of $\mathcal{F}$ can be perfectly implemented by $\mathcal{F}'$, then $\mathsf{SAT}(\mathcal{F})$ is polynomial-time reducible to $\mathsf{SAT}(\mathcal{F}')$. Given an $\mathcal{F}$-collection of constraint applications $\mathcal{C}$ on variables $\vec{x}$, replace every constraint in $\mathcal{C}$ with perfect implementation using constraints in $\mathcal{F}'$. We get an $\mathcal{F}'$-collection of constraint applications $\mathcal{C}'$ on variable set $\vec{x}, \vec{y}$, where $\vec{y}$ is the set of auxiliary variables. Since all implementations are perfect, every assignment to $\vec{x}$ that satisfies all constraints in $\mathcal{C}$ can be extended to an assignment to $\vec{x} \cup \vec{y}$ which satisfies all constraints in $\mathcal{C}'$. Conversely, given an assignment to $\vec{x} \cup \vec{y}$ that satisfies all constraints in $\mathcal{C}'$, its projection on to the primary variables $\vec{x}$ satisfies all constraints in $\mathcal{C}$. This yields the desired reduction. □

Now using the fact that $\mathsf{SAT}(\{\mathsf{OR}_{3,0}, \mathsf{OR}_{3,1}, \mathsf{OR}_{3,2}, \mathsf{OR}_{3,3}\})$ is just 3-SAT, which is NP-hard, and combining with Example 5.10, we get the following nice consequence of Lemma 5.12.

Example 5.13 *The problem* $\mathsf{SAT}(\{\mathsf{One\_in\_Three}\})$ *is* NP-*hard.*

We note here that the reduction described in Lemma 5.12 is log-space computable and thus can also be used to establish P-hardness results.

Lemma 5.14 *If* $\mathsf{SAT}(\mathcal{F}_1)$ *is* P-*hard and every constraint of* $\mathcal{F}_1$ *can be perfectly implemented by* $\mathcal{F}_2$, *then* $\mathsf{SAT}(\mathcal{F}_2)$ *is also* P-*hard.*

5.2.2 Counting problems

As for counting problems, to get #P-hardness results we use implementations that preserve the number of solutions, that is, faithful implementations.

Lemma 5.15 *If* $\#\mathsf{SAT}(\mathcal{F})$ *is* #P-*hard and every constraint of* $\mathcal{F}$ *can be faithfully implemented by* $\mathcal{F}'$, *then* $\#\mathsf{SAT}(\mathcal{F}')$ *is also* #P-*hard.*

Proof: We prove that if every constraint of $\mathcal{F}$ can be faithfully implemented by $\mathcal{F}'$, then there is a parsimonious reduction from $\#\mathsf{SAT}(\mathcal{F})$ to $\#\mathsf{SAT}(\mathcal{F}')$. As in the previous proof, we use faithful implementations to transform a given $\mathcal{F}$-collection of constraint applications on variable set $\vec{x}$, say, $\mathcal{C}$; we get an $\mathcal{F}'$-collection of constraint applications on variable set $\vec{x}, \vec{y}$, say, $\mathcal{C}'$. Since the implementations are faithful, every assignment to $\vec{x}$ satisfying all constraints in $\mathcal{C}$ can be extended in a unique way to an assignment to $\vec{x} \cup \vec{y}$ that satisfies all constraints in $\mathcal{C}'$. Therefore there is a one-to-one correspondence between the assignments to $\vec{x}$ that satisfy all constraints in $\mathcal{C}$ and the assignments to $\vec{x} \cup \vec{y}$ which satisfy all constraints in $\mathcal{C}'$. This yields the desired reduction. □

5.2.3 Quantified problems

Similar to the decision problems, we show that perfect implementations suffice for reductions among quantified problems.

Lemma 5.16 *If* QSAT$(\mathcal{F})$ *is* PSPACE-*hard and every constraint of* $\mathcal{F}$ *can be perfectly implemented by* $\mathcal{F}'$, *then* QSAT$(\mathcal{F}')$ *is also* PSPACE-*hard.*

Proof: We prove that if every constraint of $\mathcal{F}$ can be perfectly implemented by $\mathcal{F}'$, then QSAT$(\mathcal{F})$ is log-space reducible to $\mathcal{F}'$. Let $\mathcal{Q}_1 x_1 \ldots \mathcal{Q}_n x_n \mathcal{C}$ be a quantified $\mathcal{F}$-expression on variable set $\vec{x} = \{x_1, \ldots, x_n\}$. Replace every constraint in $\mathcal{C}$ with perfect implementations using constraints of $\mathcal{F}'$; thus we get $\mathcal{C}'$ on variables set $\vec{x}, \vec{y}$. Finally, consider the following quantified expression:

$$\mathcal{Q}_1 x_1 \ldots \mathcal{Q}_n x_n \exists \vec{y} \; \mathcal{C}'.$$

Since the implementations are perfect, it is clear that the initial quantified $\mathcal{F}$-expression is true if and only if the expression above is true. This yields the desired reduction. □

5.3 Reductions for optimization problems

In this section we show that implementations lead to reductions for optimization problems. In the case of MAX SAT and MIN SAT, this holds for unweighted problems as well as weighted problems. In the case of MIN ONES and MAX ONES, the reductions work only when one is allowed to use weights. It turns out, however, that weights do not play any significant role in determining the approximability behavior of these problems. This issue will be dealt with in Chapter 7.

5.3.1 Reductions for MAX SAT problems

We first show how strict implementations are useful in establishing AP-reducibility among MAX SAT problems. We need a simple statement about the approximability of MAX SAT problems.

Proposition 5.17 [74] *For every constraint family* $\mathcal{F}$ *(with no unsatisfiable constraints) there exists a positive constant* β *such that given any instance* $\mathcal{I}$ *of* MAX SAT$(\mathcal{F})$ *with* m *constraint applications, a solution satisfying* m/β *constraints can be found in polynomial time. Moreover, the statement also holds for* Weighted MAX SAT$(\mathcal{F})$.

Proof: The proposition follows from the proof of Theorem 1 in [74] which shows the above for every "MAX SNP problem." (MAX SNP is a class of optimization problems introduced in [74]. This class contains every MAX SAT$(\mathcal{F})$ problem.)

Briefly, their proof, specialized to MAX SAT$(\mathcal{F})$, goes as follows: Let k be the maximum arity of a constraint in $\mathcal{F}$ and let $\beta = 2^k$. Then for any instance of MAX SAT$(\mathcal{F})$ on m constraints, a random assignment satisfies a given constraint application with probability at least $1/\beta$, and hence is expected to satisfy at least m/β constraints. Thus every instance on m constraints has an assignment satisfying at least m/β constraints. Further, such an assignment can be found deterministically using the "method of conditional probabilities" (see, for instance, [72]).

The result for the weighted case is completely analogous. □

Lemma 5.18 *If every constraint of $\mathcal{F}$ can be strictly implemented by $\mathcal{F}'$, then* MAX SAT$(\mathcal{F})$ *is AP-reducible to* MAX SAT$(\mathcal{F}')$.

Proof: Our reduction uses Proposition 5.17 above. Let β a constant such that given an instance $\mathcal{I}$ of MAX SAT$(\mathcal{F})$ with m constraints an assignment satisfying $\frac{m}{\beta}$ constraints can be found in polynomial time.

Recall that we need to show polynomial time constructible functions f and g such that f maps an instance $\mathcal{I}$ of MAX SAT$(\mathcal{F})$ to an instance of MAX SAT$(\mathcal{F}')$, and g maps a solution to $f(\mathcal{I})$ back to a solution of $\mathcal{I}$. Given an instance $\mathcal{I}$ on n variables and m constraints, the mapping f simply replaces every constraint application in $\mathcal{I}$ with a strict α-implementation using constraints of $\mathcal{F}'$, for some constant α. (Notice that by Lemma 5.11, such an α does exist.) The mapping retains the original n variables of $\mathcal{I}$ as primary variables and uses m independent copies of the auxiliary variables; one independent copy for every constraint in $\mathcal{I}$.

Let $\langle s_x, s_y \rangle$ be an r-approximate solution to the instance $f(\mathcal{I})$, where s_x denotes the assignment to the original variables $\vec{x}$ of $\mathcal{I}$ and s_y denotes the assignment to the auxiliary variables $\vec{y}$ introduced in the implementations. The mapping g uses two possible solutions and takes the better of the two. The first solution is simply s_x, while the second solution $s_{x'}$ is a solution that satisfies at least m/β of the constraints in $\mathcal{I}$ (existence is guaranteed by Proposition 5.17). The function g outputs the better of the two solutions.

We now show that a r-approximate solution leads to an r'-approximate solution, where $r' \leq 1 + \gamma(r-1)$ for some constant γ. Let OPT denote the optimum value for the instance $\mathcal{I}$. Then the optimum value for the instance $f(\mathcal{I})$ is exactly OPT$+m(\alpha-1)$. This computation uses the fact that for every satisfied constraint in the optimal assignment to $\mathcal{I}$, we can satisfy α constraints of its implementation by choosing the auxiliary variables appropriately (from properties (a) and (b) of Definition 5.1); and for every unsatisfied constraint exactly $\alpha - 1$ constraints of its implementation can be satisfied (from property (c) and strictness of the implementation). Thus the solution $\langle s_x, s_y \rangle$ satisfies at least $\frac{1}{r}($OPT$+m(\alpha-1))$ constraints of $f(\mathcal{I})$, and hence x satisfies at least $\frac{1}{r}($OPT$+m(\alpha-1))-m(\alpha-1)$ constraints in $\mathcal{I}$. Note that here we use properties (a) and (c) of Definition 5.1 to see that there must be at least $\frac{1}{r}($OPT$+m(\alpha-1))-m(\alpha-1)$ constraints of $\mathcal{I}$ in whose implementations exactly α constraints must be satisfied. Thus the solution output by g satisfies at least

$$\max \left\{ \frac{1}{r}(\text{OPT} + m(\alpha - 1)) - m(\alpha - 1), \frac{m}{\beta} \right\}$$

constraints. Using the fact that $\max\{a, b\} \geq \lambda a + (1 - \lambda)b$ for any $\lambda \in [0, 1]$ and using $\lambda = \frac{r}{r + \beta(\alpha-1)(r-1)}$, we lower bound the above expression by

$$\frac{\text{OPT}}{r + \beta(\alpha - 1)(r - 1)}.$$

Thus

$$r' \leq \frac{\text{OPT}}{\text{OPT}/(r + \beta(\alpha - 1)(r - 1))} = r + \beta(\alpha - 1)(r - 1) = 1 + (\beta(\alpha - 1) + 1)(r - 1).$$

Hence g maps r-approximate solutions of $f(\mathcal{I})$ to $1 + \gamma(r - 1)$ approximate solutions to $\mathcal{I}$ for $\gamma = \beta(\alpha - 1) + 1 < \infty$ as required. $\square$

Corollary 5.19 *If* MAX SAT$(\mathcal{F})$ *is APX-hard and every constraint of $\mathcal{F}$ can be strictly implemented by $\mathcal{F}'$, then* MAX SAT$(\mathcal{F}')$ *is also APX-hard.*

5.3.2   Reductions for MAX ONES and MIN ONES problems

Since every feasible solution to a MAX ONES (MIN ONES) problem must satisfy all constraint applications, it is natural to consider perfect implementations. We now show that perfect implementations can be used to establish AP-reducibility for these problems.

Lemma 5.20 *If every constraint of $\mathcal{F}$ can be perfectly implements by $\mathcal{F}'$, then* Weighted MAX ONES($\mathcal{F}$) *is AP-reducible to* Weighted MAX ONES($\mathcal{F}'$). *An analogous result holds for* Weighted MIN ONES($\mathcal{F}$).

Proof: Again we need to show polynomial time constructible functions f and g such that f maps an instance $\mathcal{I}$ of Weighted MAX ONES($\mathcal{F}$) (Weighted MIN ONES($\mathcal{F}$)) to an instance of Weighted MAX ONES($\mathcal{F}'$) (Weighted MIN ONES($\mathcal{F}$)), and g maps a solution to $f(\mathcal{I})$ back to a solution of $\mathcal{I}$.

Given an instance $\mathcal{I}$ on n variables and m constraints, the mapping f simply replaces every constraint in $\mathcal{I}$ (which belongs to $\mathcal{F}$) with perfect implementations using constraints of $\mathcal{F}'$. The mapping retains the original n variables of $\mathcal{I}$ as primary variables and uses m independent copies of the auxiliary variables; one independent copy for every constraint in $\mathcal{I}$. Further, $f(\mathcal{I})$ retains the weight of the primary variables from $\mathcal{I}$ and associates a weight of zero to all the newly created auxiliary variables. Given a solution to $f(\mathcal{I})$, the mapping g is simply the projection of the solution back to the primary variables. It is clear that every feasible solution to $\mathcal{I}$ can be extended into a feasible solution to $f(\mathcal{I})$ which preserves the value of the objective; alternatively, the mapping g maps feasible solutions to $f(\mathcal{I})$ into feasible solutions to $\mathcal{I}$ with the same objective. (This is where the perfectness of the implementations is being used.) Thus the optimum of $f(\mathcal{I})$ equals the value of the optimum of $\mathcal{I}$ and given an r-approximate solution to $f(\mathcal{I})$, the mapping g yields an r-approximate solution to $\mathcal{I}$.   □

Corollary 5.21 *If* Weighted MAX ONES($\mathcal{F}$) *is APX-hard and $\mathcal{F}'$ perfectly implements every constraint in $\mathcal{F}$, then* Weighted MAX ONES($\mathcal{F}'$) *is APX-hard. Similarly, if* Weighted MAX ONES($\mathcal{F}$) *is poly-APX-hard and $\mathcal{F}'$ perfectly implements every constraint in $\mathcal{F}$, then weighted* Weighted MAX ONES($\mathcal{F}'$) *is poly-APX-hard. Analogous results hold for* Weighted MIN ONES *as well.*

5.3.3   Reductions for MIN SAT

Lemma 5.22 *If every constraint of $\mathcal{F}$ is perfectly implemented by $\mathcal{F}'$, then* MIN SAT($\mathcal{F}$) *is A-reducible to* MIN SAT($\mathcal{F}'$).

Proof: Let α be large enough so that any constraint from $\mathcal{F}$ has a perfect α-implementation using constraints from $\mathcal{F}'$. Let $\mathcal{I}$ be an instance of MIN SAT($\mathcal{F}$) and let $\mathcal{I}'$ be the instance of MIN SAT($\mathcal{F}'$) obtained by replacing each constraint of $\mathcal{I}$ with the respective k-implementation. Once again each implementation uses the original set of variables for its primary variables and uses its own independent copy of the auxiliary variables. It is easy to check that any assigment for $\mathcal{I}'$ of cost V yields an assigment for $\mathcal{I}$ whose cost is between V/α and V. It is immediate to check that if the former solution is r-approximate, then the latter is (αr)-approximate.   □

5.4 Implementation results: Classical and new

In this section we present results about how function families that do not possess a given property implement some elementary functions that lack the same property. Since the section is somewhat long, it may be useful to anticipate some of the results. Let us consider some of the simplest examples of functions that do not possess a given property. (The notion of "simplicity" here is just that we consider a function of the smallest possible arity that does not possess a given property). For non-0-validity, the function $T(x)$ is a good example. Similarly, for non-1-validity, the function $F(x)$ is a good example. Continuing in this manner, we obtain the following examples:

- Non-affine: the functions OR_0, OR_1 and OR_2 are non-affine.

- Non-bijunctive: any of the ternary functions listed in Chapter 3, including $OR_{3,j}$, XOR_3 and One_in_Three.

- Non-weakly-positive/weakly-negative: the functions $OR_{3,2}$ and $OR_{3,3}$ are not weakly positive, while $OR_{3,0}$ and $OR_{3,1}$ are not weakly negative.

- Affine, but not width 2: the functions XOR_3 and $XNOR_3$ are affine but not of width 2.

- Non-2-monotone: the function XOR is not 2-monotone.

Surprisingly, it turns out that whenever a constraint family does not have one of the properties listed above, then the family implements (sometimes with help) one of the corresponding example functions listed above. Thus these example functions serve as the unifying theme for all constraint families that lack a given property. As we will see later, this unification is central to our classification results.

5.4.1 Preliminaries

We start by first showing that implementations do not enhance the power of a function family by much. In particular all properties defined in Chapter 4 are closed under appropriate forms of implementations. The following lemma illustrates closure under perfect implementations.

Lemma 5.23 *If $\mathcal{F}$ is a weakly positive (weakly negative / bijunctive / IHS-B+/ IHS-B−) family and $\mathcal{F}$ perfectly implements f, then f is also weakly positive (weakly negative / bijunctive / IHS-B+/ IHS-B−).*

Proof: Let $f(x_1, \ldots, x_k)$ be perfectly implemented by the collection of constraint applications $f_1, \ldots, f_m$ with f_j being applied to some subset of the primary variables $x_1, \ldots, x_k$ and the auxiliary variables $y_1, \ldots, y_l$. Fix $j \in \{1, \ldots, m\}$ and consider the constraint function $f'_j(x_1, \ldots, x_k, y_1, \ldots, y_l)$ which is satisfied by an assignment to $\vec{x}, \vec{y}$ if and only if the jth constraint application f_j is satisfied. Notice that f'_j is a weakly positive constraint (though it may not necessarily lie in $\mathcal{F}$ due to syntactic reasons). Now consider the function $f'(\vec{x}, \vec{y}) = \wedge_{j=1}^{m} f'_j(\vec{x}, \vec{y})$. Since f' is the conjunction of weakly positive functions, f' also weakly positive. Now $f(x_1, \ldots, x_k)$ is simply the function $\exists \vec{y}$ s.t. $f'(\vec{x}, \vec{y})$. By Lemma 4.5, f is also weakly positive. □

Similar results hold true also for perfect implementations obtained from affine families and affine famiens with width two. Similarly strict implementations obtained from 2-monotone families only give rise to 2-monotone functions. These results are implicit from this monograph, but not derived explicitly here.

5.4.2   Non-0-valid and non-1-valid functions

First let us observe that as soon as we have the functions F and T we can freely use the constants 0 and 1 since we can get rid of them by replacing them by two new variables x_0 and x_1 and by adding the constraints $\mathsf{F}(x_0)$ and $\mathsf{T}(x_1)$.

Lemma 5.24 *If $\mathcal{F}$ is not 0-valid (1-valid) and*

1. *if $\mathcal{F}$ is C-closed, then $\mathcal{F}$ implements XOR strictly, perfectly and faithfully.*

2. *if $\mathcal{F}$ is not C-closed, then $\mathcal{F}$ implements T (F) strictly, perfectly and faithfully.*

Proof: Let $f \in \mathcal{F}$ be non-0-valid. If f is C-closed, then f is also not 1-valid. Let s be a satisfying assignment for f. Observe that both $O(s)$ and $Z(s)$ are non-empty. Consider the constraint $g(x, y)$ obtained from f by substituting the variable x for all variables in $O(s)$ and the variable y for all variables in $Z(s)$. Since $f(\vec{0}) = f(\vec{1}) = 0$ and $f(s) = f(\bar{s}) = 1$, we find that $g(x, y) = x \oplus y$. This yields part 1 of the lemma.

For part 2, we consider several cases. Again let f be a non-0-valid function in $\mathcal{F}$. If f is 1-valid then the constraint obtained from f by substituting the variable x for all variables of f is the constraint $\mathsf{T}(x)$ as required. Otherwise, f is not 1-valid. Again if f is not C-closed, then there is an assignment s different from $\vec{0}$ and $\vec{1}$ such that $f(s) = 1$ and $f(\bar{s}) = 0$. Consider the constraint $g(x, y)$ obtained from f by substituting x for all variables in $Z(s)$ and y for all variables in $O(s)$. Then $g(x, y) = \bar{x} \wedge y$ and thus the constraint $\exists x$ s.t. $g(x, y)$ implements $\mathsf{T}(y)$. Finally we are left with the case when f is C-closed. (But $\mathcal{F}$ is not!) In this case, f implements XOR. Let h be a non-C-closed function in $\mathcal{F}$ with $h(s) = 1$ and $h(\bar{s}) = 0$. Substituting x for all variables in $O(s)$ and y for all variables in $Z(s)$ we get a function $g(x, y)$ with $g(10) = 1$ and $g(01) = 0$. Now the constraints $g(x, y)$ and $\mathsf{XOR}(x, y)$ give strict, perfect and faithful 2-implementation of $\mathsf{T}(x)$, concluding this case also.   □

5.4.3   Non-C-closed functions

The following lemma is a dual to the last one, in that it assumes a family is not C-closed and then describes what can be implemented with it, depending on whether or not it is 0-valid or 1-valid.

Lemma 5.25 [19] *Let $\mathcal{F}$ be a non-C-closed family.*

1. *If $\mathcal{F}$ is both 0-valid and 1-valid, then $\mathcal{F}$ implements OR_1 strictly, faithfully and perfectly.*

2. *If $\mathcal{F}$ is not 0-valid (resp., not 1-valid), then $\mathcal{F}$ implements T (resp., F) strictly, perfectly and faithfully.*

Proof: Part 2 is identical to Lemma 5.24, part 2. For part 1, let $f \in \mathcal{F}$ be non-C-closed. Let s be an assignment such that $f(s) = 1$ and $f(\bar{s}) = 0$. Let $g(x, y)$ be obtained from f by substituting x for all variables in $O(s)$ and y for all variables in $Z(s)$. Since f is 0-valid and 1-valid, the function $g(x, y)$ is given by $g(00) = g(10) = g(11) = 1$ and $g(01) = 0$. In other words, $g(x, y) = x \wedge \bar{y}$, which gives part 1.   □

5.4.4 Non-weakly-negative and non-weakly-positive functions

Lemma 5.26 [82, 54] *Let f_+ be a non-weakly-positive function and f_- be a non-weakly-negative function. Then*

1. $\{f_+, \mathsf{F}, \mathsf{T}\}$ *implements at least one of* XOR *or* OR_2 *strictly, perfectly and faithfully.*

2. $\{f_-, \mathsf{F}, \mathsf{T}\}$ *implements at least one of* XOR *or* OR_0 *strictly, perfectly and faithfully.*

3. $\{f_+, f_-, \mathsf{F}, \mathsf{T}\}$ *implements* XOR *strictly, perfectly and faithfully.*

Proof: We first show that $\{f_-, \mathsf{F}, \mathsf{T}\})$ can implement either the function XOR or the function OR_0. By Lemma 4.8, there are two satisfying assignments for f_-, say s_1 and s_2, such that $s_1 \cap s_2$ is not a satisfying assignment. Observe that both $O(s_1) \cap Z(s_2)$ and $Z(s_1) \cap O(s_2)$ are non-empty. Consider the constraint $C(u, x, y, v)$ obtained from f_- by assigning an identical value u to all variables in $Z(s_1) \cap Z(s_2)$, an identical value x to all variables in $Z(s_1) \cap O(s_2)$, an identical value y to all variables in $O(s_1) \cap Z(s_2)$ and an identical value v to all variables in $O(s_1) \cap O(s_2)$. It is easy to see that the set of constraints $\{C(u, x, y, v), \mathsf{F}(u), \mathsf{T}(v)\}$ strictly, perfectly, and faithfully implements either the function $\mathsf{XOR}(x, y)$ or $\mathsf{OR}_0(x, y)$ depending on whether $s_1 \cup s_2$ is satisfying. Similarly, we can show that $\{f_+, \mathsf{F}, \mathsf{T}\})$ can strictly, perfectly, and faithfully implement either the function XOR or the function OR_2. Finally, since $\{\mathsf{OR}_0, \mathsf{OR}_2\}$ can strictly, perfectly, and faithfully implement XOR, we conclude that $\{f_+, f_-, \mathsf{F}, \mathsf{T}\}$ can strictly, perfectly, and faithfully implement XOR. □

5.4.5 Non-IHS-B functions

Lemma 5.27 *If f is a weakly negative (weakly positive) function which is not IHS-$B-$ (IHS-$B+$), then $\{f, \mathsf{F}, \mathsf{T}\}$ can perfectly implement the function $\mathsf{OR}_{3,2}$ ($\mathsf{OR}_{3,1}$).*

Proof: We know that f has a maxterm m with one positive literal and at least two negative literals. Let us assume that $m = (x \vee \bar{y} \vee \bar{z} \vee \ldots)$. Consider the function $f'(x, y, z)$ which is f existentially quantified over the variables not in m with all variables in m different from x, y and z set (with the functions F and T) to the value which does not make m true. Then the assignment $x = 0$, $y = z = 1$ is a non-satisfying assignment, $f'(011) = 0$. By the definition of a maxterm $f'(010) = f'(001) = f'(111) = 1$. Moreover, $(0, 0, 0) = (0, 1, 0) \cap (0, 0, 1)$, and since f' is a weakly negative constraint $f'(000) = 1$ (Lemma 4.8). Finally, the following values of f' are undetermined $A = f'(100)$, $B = f'(101)$ and $C = f'(110)$. Observe that $(1, 0, 0) = (1, 0, 1) \cap (1, 1, 0)$ and remind that f' is a weakly negative constraint. Therefore we cannot have $B = C = 1$ and $A = 0$ (Lemma 4.8). It remains several cases to discuss.

If $A = 1$, then $(x \vee \bar{y} \vee \bar{z}) \equiv \exists u_1 f'(x, u_1, u_1) \wedge f'(u_1, y, z)$.
If $A = B = 0$, then $(x \vee \bar{y} \vee \bar{z}) \equiv \exists u_1 \exists u_2 \exists u_3 \exists u_4 f'(x, u_1, u_2) \wedge f'(y, u_1, u_3) \wedge f'(z, u_2, u_4)$.
If $A = C = 0$, then $(x \vee \bar{y} \vee \bar{z}) \equiv \exists u_1 \exists u_2 \exists u_3 \exists u_4 f'(x, u_1, u_2) \wedge f'(y, u_3, u_1) \wedge f'(z, u_4, u_2)$.

Therefore, in any case, $\{f, \mathsf{T}, \mathsf{F}\}$ can perfectly implement the function $\mathsf{OR}_{3,2}$. □

Lemma 5.28 *If f is affine with width two which is not IHS-$B-$ or IHS-$B+$, then $\{f, \mathsf{F}, \mathsf{T}\}$ perfectly implements the function XOR.*

Proof: By Lemmas 5.26 and 5.27, we have that $\{f, \mathsf{F}, \mathsf{T}\}$ strictly, perfectly and faithfully implements at least one of the functions in the set $\{\mathsf{XOR}, \mathsf{OR}_0, \mathsf{OR}_2, \mathsf{OR}_{3,1}, \mathsf{OR}_{3,2}\}$. (If f is weakly positive or negative, we get one of the last two, else we get one of the first three.) But the last four functions in this set are not affine with width 2, and by Lemma 5.23, a width-2 affine family can only implement functions that are width-2 affine. Hence $\{f, \mathsf{F}, \mathsf{T}\}$ must implement XOR strictly, perfectly and faithfully. □

Lemma 5.29 *If f is bijunctive but not IHS-B− or IHS-B+, then $\{f, \mathsf{F}, \mathsf{T}\}$ strictly, perfectly and faithfully implements the functions XOR or $\{f, \mathsf{F}, \mathsf{T}\}$ strictly, perfectly and faithfully implements both the functions OR_0 and OR_2.*

Proof: Examining Lemmas 5.26 and 5.27, more carefully now, we have that $\{f, \mathsf{F}, \mathsf{T}\}$ strictly, perfectly and faithfully implements all the functions from at least one of the three families: $\mathcal{F}_1 = \{OR_0, OR_2\}$, $\mathcal{F}_2 = \{XOR\}$, or $\mathcal{F}_3 = \{OR_{3,1}, OR_{3,2}\}$. In the first two cases we are done. In the third case, we use the fact that $OR_{3,1}(x, y, z) \wedge \mathsf{F}(z)$ gives a strict, perfect and faithful implementation of $OR_0(y, z)$ (and similarly for OR_2). Thus in this case also we get a strict, perfect and faithful implementation of $\{OR_0, OR_2\}$. □

5.4.6 Non-affine functions

We now turn our attention to non-affine functions. The following lemma shows that, with the help of either F or T, they implement one of the three functions OR_0, OR_1, or OR_2. Notice that these are the only three non-affine functions on up to two variables!

Lemma 5.30 *If f is not affine, then $\{f, \mathsf{F}\}$ ($\{f, \mathsf{T}\}$) implements at least one of the three functions OR_0, OR_1 or OR_2 strictly, perfectly and faithfully. Furthermore, if f is 0-valid (1-valid), then $\{f, \mathsf{F}\}$ ($\{f, \mathsf{T}\}$) implements one of OR_1 or OR_2 (OR_0 or OR_1) strictly, perfectly and faithfully*

Proof: We start by considering the case when f is 0-valid (the case 1-valid is similar). In this case, by Lemma 4.10, there exist assignments s_1, s_2 such that $f(s_1) = f(s_2) = 1$, but $f(s_1 \oplus s_2) = 0$. The following table describes the situation:

					$f()$
	00...0	00...0	00...0	00...0	1
s_1	00...0	00...0	11...1	11...1	1
s_2	00...0	11...1	00...0	11...1	1
$s_1 \oplus s_2$	00...0	11...1	11...1	00...0	0
	00...0	$xx...x$	$yy...y$	$zz...z$	

Fixing the above variables to 0's as shown in the last row, and assigning replicated copies of three variables x, y and z, we get a constraint $h(x, y, z)$, such that $h(000) = h(011) = h(101) = 1$ and $h(110) = 0$. (Notice that forcing variables to 0 is feasible since the constraint F is available.) In Claim 5.31 we prove that for any such function h the family $\{h, \mathsf{F}\}$ implements at least one of OR_1 or OR_2 strictly, perfectly and faithfully.

We now move to the case where f is not 0-valid. Observe that in this case $\{f, \mathsf{F}\}$ can implement T strictly, perfectly and faithfully. (Let s be a satisfying assignment. Let $g(x, y)$ be the constraint obtained from f by substituting the variable x for all variables in $O(s)$ and the variable y for all variables in $Z(s)$. The set of constraints $\{g(x, y), \mathsf{F}(y)\}$ gives a strict, perfect and faithful implementation of $T(x)$.) Therefore, we prove that $\{f, \mathsf{F}, \mathsf{T}\}$ can implement one of OR_0, OR_1 or OR_2 strictly, perfectly and faithfully. Here again we get into two cases depending on whether f is weakly negative. First, if f is weakly negative. Let

s_0 be the assignment defined by $s_0 = \bigcap_{s \ satisfies \ f} s$. Following Lemma 4.8, s_0 satisfies f. According to Lemma 4.10 there exist two assignments s_1, s_2 that satisfy f such that $f(s_0 \oplus s_1 \oplus s_2) = 0$. By definition of s_0, our situation is summarized by the following table.

						$f()$
s_0	00...0	00...0	00...0	00...0	11...1	0
s_1	00...0	00...0	11...1	11...1	11...1	1
s_2	00...0	11...1	00...0	11...1	11...1	1
$s_1 \oplus s_2$	00...0	11...1	11...1	00...0	11...1	1
	00...0	$xx...x$	$yy...y$	$zz...z$	11...1	

Thus, forcing the variables to $0, x, y, z$ or 1 as described in the last row, we get a function h with $h(000) = h(011) = h(101) = 1$ and $h(110) = 0$. (Notice that forcing variables to 0 or 1 is feasible since both the constraints F and T are available.) Applying Claim 5.31 we find that in this case $\{h, \mathsf{F}, \mathsf{T}\}$ implements one of OR_1 or OR_2 strictly, perfectly and faithfully.

Next we consider the case when f is neither 0-valid nor weakly negative. Following Lemma 5.26 $\{f, \mathsf{F}, \mathsf{T}\}$ implements at least one of OR_0 or XOR strictly, perfectly and faithfully. In the first case, we are done, so we consider the second.

At this stage it suffices to show that $\{f, \mathsf{XOR}, \mathsf{F}, \mathsf{T}\}$ implement one of the three functions OR_0, OR_1 or OR_2, for a non-affine function f. Using Lemma 4.10 we know there exist assignments s_1, s_2, s_3 satisfying f such that $s_1 \oplus s_2 \oplus s_3$ does not satisfy f. The situation is summarized below.

									$f()$
s_1	00...0	00...0	00...0	00...0	11...1	11...1	11...1	11...1	1
s_2	00...0	00...0	11...1	11...1	00...0	00...0	11...1	11...1	1
s_3	00...0	11...1	00...0	11...1	00...0	11...1	00...0	11...1	1
$s_1 \oplus s_2 \oplus s_3$	00...0	11...1	11...1	00...0	11...1	00...0	00...0	11...1	0
	00...0	$xx...x$	$yy...y$	$zz...z$	$\bar{z}\bar{z}...\bar{z}$	$\bar{y}\bar{y}...\bar{y}$	$\bar{x}\bar{x}...\bar{x}$	11...1	

Thus, creating a 6-ary function $h(x, y, z, \bar{x}, \bar{y}, \bar{z})$ using the usual substitutions, and then adding the constraints $\mathsf{XOR}(x, \bar{x})$, $\mathsf{XOR}(y, \bar{y})$ and $\mathsf{XOR}(z, \bar{z})$, we get a perfect, strict and faithful implementation of a function h' with $h'(000) = h'(011) = h'(101) = 1$ and $h'(110) = 0$. Once again applying Claim 5.31 we find that $\{h', \mathsf{F}, \mathsf{T}\}$ implements one of the functions OR_1 or OR_2 strictly, perfectly and faithfully. $\qquad\square$

To conclude the proof of Lemma 5.30, we still need the following claim.

Claim 5.31 *Let h be a ternary function with $h(000) = h(011) = h(101) = 1$ and $h(110) = 0$. Then $\{h, \mathsf{F}\}$ implements OR_1 or OR_2 strictly, perfectly and faithfully.*

Proof: Let $A = h(001)$, $B = h(010)$, $C = h(100)$ and $D = h(111)$ be the undetermined values of h. The following analysis shows that for every possible values of A, B, C and D we can implement either OR_1 or OR_2 strictly, perfectly and faithfully.

If $B = 0$ and $D = 1$, $h(x, y, x) = (x \vee \bar{y})$.
If $B = 1$ and $D = 0$, $h(x, y, x) = (\bar{x} \vee \bar{y})$.
If $C = 0$ and $D = 1$, $h(x, y, y) = (\bar{x} \vee y)$.
If $C = 1$ and $D = 0$, $h(x, y, y) = (\bar{x} \vee \bar{y})$.
If $B = C = 1$, $h(x, y, z) \wedge \mathsf{F}(z) = (\bar{x} \vee \bar{y}) \wedge \mathsf{F}(z)$.
If $B = C = D = 0$ and $A = 0$, $h(x, y, z) = \exists! x$ s. t. $(\bar{y} \vee z)$.
If $B = C = D = 0$ and $A = 1$, $h(x, y, z) \wedge \mathsf{F}(x) = (\bar{y} \vee z) \wedge \mathsf{F}(x)$. $\qquad\square$

5.4.7   Non-bijunctive functions

Lemma 5.32 [82] *For any $i \in \{0, 1, 2\}$, $\{OR_i, XOR\}$ can perfectly implement each of OR_0, OR_1 and OR_2.*

Proof: We consider the case $i = 0$; the other cases are analogous. The constraint set $\{OR_0(x', y), XOR(x', x)\}$ perfectly implements the constraint $OR_1(x, y)$, while the constraint $OR_2(x, y)$ is perfectly implemented by the constraint set $\{OR_0(x', y'), XOR(x', x), XOR(y', y)\}$.   □

Lemma 5.33 [82] *If f is not bijunctive, then $\{f, F, T, OR_0, OR_1, OR_2\}$ can perfectly implement the function* One_in_Three.

Proof: If f is not bijunctive, then in the CNF representation of f, there must be a maxterm m with at least three literals. Without loss of generality, let us assume that $m = (x \vee y \vee z \vee \ldots)$. Using the functions F and T, we can force all the remaining literals in m to false, and existentially quantifying over the remaining variables gives us a function f' with a maxterm $m' = (x \vee y \vee z)$. By the definition of maxterm, f' must be satisfiable by any assignment which sets exactly one of the x, y and z to true.

Now consider the constraints $\{f'(x, y, z), OR_2(x, y), OR_2(y, z), OR_2(x, z)\}$. Clearly, all constraints are satisfied if and only if exactly one of the x, y and z are set to true. This completes the proof.   □

5.4.8   Affine functions not of width 2

Lemma 5.34 *If f is an affine function which is not of width-2, then f strictly and perfectly implements* XNOR$_4$.

Proof: Let k be the arity of f. Recall the notion of a dependent set of variables. A set S of variables is dependent if not every assignment to the variables in S extends to a satisfying assignment of f. A dependent set S is minimally dependent set if no strict subset $S' \subset S$ is a dependent set. Notice that f can be expressed as the conjunction of constraints on its minimally dependent sets. Thus, following Lemma 4.11, if f is not of width-2, then it must have a minimally dependent set S of cardinality at least 3. Assume $S = \{1, \ldots, p\}$, where $p \geq 3$. Consider the function

$$f_1(x_1 \ldots x_p) = \exists x_{p+1}, \ldots, x_k \text{ s.t. } f(x_1, \ldots x_k).$$

f_1 is affine (by Lemma 4.5), is not satisfied by every assignment and has at least 2^{p-1} satisfying assignments. Thus f_1 has exactly 2^{p-1} assignments (since the number of satisfying assignments must be a power of 2). Thus f_1 is described by exactly one linear constraint and by the minimality of S this must be the constraint $XOR_p(x_1 \ldots x_p)$ or the constraint $XNOR_p(x_1 \ldots x_p)$. Now setting $x_4 = x_5 = \cdots = x_p$, we get an implementation of one of the constraints $XOR_3(x_1, x_2, x_3)$, $XOR_4(x_1, x_2, x_3, x_4)$, $XNOR_3(x_1, x_2, x_3)$ or $XNOR_4(x_1, x_2, x_3, x_4)$.

We conclude by showing that in any of the first 3 cases, we can implement the constraint $XNOR_4$. Notice that $XOR_3(x_1, x_2, y)$ and $XOR_3(y, x_3, x_4)$ give a strict and perfect implementation of $XNOR_4(x_1, x_2, x_3, x_4)$. Similarly $XNOR_3(x_1, x_2, y)$ and $XNOR_3(y, x_3, x_4)$ also give a strict and perfect implementation of $XNOR_4(x_1, x_2, x_3, x_4)$. Finally, $XOR_4(x_1, x_2, y, z)$ and $XOR_4(y, z, x_3, x_4)$ give a strict and perfect implementation of $XNOR_4(x_1, x_2, x_3, x_4)$. Thus in all cases we may implement $XNOR_4$ strictly and perfectly.   □

5.4.9 Non-2-monotone functions

Lemma 5.35 *For any $f \in \{x \vee y, x \wedge \bar{y}, \bar{x} \vee \bar{y}\}$, $\{f, \mathsf{F}, \mathsf{T}\}$ strictly implements the* XOR *constraint.*

Proof: If $f = x \vee y$, then the instance $\{f(x, y), f(y, x), \mathsf{F}(x), \mathsf{F}(y)\}$ is a strict 3-implementation of $x \oplus y$; if $f = x \wedge \bar{y}$, then the instance $\{f(x, y), f(y, x)\}$ is a strict 1-implementation of $x \oplus y$; and finally, if $f = \bar{x} \vee \bar{y}$, then $\{f(x, y), f(y, x), \mathsf{T}(x), \mathsf{T}(y)\}$ is a strict 3-implementation of $x \oplus y$. □

Lemma 5.36 [54] *For any function f which is not 2-monotone, $\{f, \mathsf{F}, \mathsf{T}\}$ can strictly implement the function* XOR.

Proof: We prove this by using the Lemma 4.13 for 2-monotone constraints. Let k denote the arity of f. If f is not 2-monotone, it must violate one of the three conditions (a), (b) and (c) stated in the Lemma 4.13.

Suppose f violates the property (a) of Lemma 4.13. Then for some satisfying assignment s, there exist two assignments s_0 and s_1 such that $Z(s) \subset Z(s_0)$ and $O(s) \subset O(s_1)$, but $f(s_0) = f(s_1) = 0$. Without loss of generality, we assume that $s = 0^p 1^q$, $s_0 = 0^{p+a} 1^{q-a}$ and $s_1 = 0^{p-b} 1^{q+b}$, where $p + q = k$. Thus we have the following situation:

	$\overbrace{p-a}$	$\overbrace{a}$	$\overbrace{b}$	$\overbrace{q-b}$	$f()$
s	00...0	00...0	11...1	11...1	1
s_0	00...0	00...0	00...0	11...1	0
s_1	00...0	11...1	11...1	11...1	0
s_2	00...0	11...1	00...0	11...1	_
	00...0	$xx...x$	$yy...y$	11...1	_

Observe that both a and b are non-zero. Fixing the above variables to 0 and 1 as shown in the last row and assigning the variables x and y we get a constraint $h(x, y)$.

Let s_2 be the assignment as defined in the preceding table. It is easy to verify that this is a strict implementation of the constraint $x \oplus y$ if $f(s_2) = 1$ and the constraint $x \wedge \bar{y}$, otherwise. The claim now follows immediately from Lemma 5.35.

Next suppose f violates the property (b) of Lemma 4.13. Then there exists an unsatisfying assignment s to f satisfying $V_1 \cap V_2 \subset O(s)$. Notice that $O(s)$ cannot contain V_1 or V_2 (since V_1 and V_2 are 1-consistent for f). Thus, s sets all variables in $V_1 \cap V_2$ to 1 and at least one variable in each of $V_1 \setminus (V_1 \cap V_2)$ and $V_2 \setminus (V_1 \cap V_2)$ to 0. Consider one such unsatisfying assignment s. Without loss of generality, we have the following situation:

	$\overbrace{V_1 \setminus O(s)}$		$\overbrace{V_1 \cap V_2}$		$\overbrace{V_2 \setminus O(s)}$		
s	00...0	11...1	11...1	11...1	00...0	00...0	11...1
	p	q	r	t	u	v	w
	$xx..x$	11..1	11..1	11..1	$yy..y$	00..0	11..1

with V_1 spanning $V_1 \setminus O(s)$, $V_1 \cap V_2$ and V_2 spanning $V_1 \cap V_2$, $V_2 \setminus O(s)$.

Fixing the above variables to 0 and 1 as shown in the last row and assigning the variables x and y we get a constraint $h(x, y)$. It is now easy to verify that this is a strict

α-implementation of the constraint $x \vee y$. Again, the claim now follows immediately from Lemma 5.35.

Finally, the case in which f violates the property (c) above, can be handled in an analogous manner. $\square$

Lemma 5.37 [54] *Let f_0 be a constraint that is not 0-valid, f_1 be a constraint that is not 1-valid and f_2 be a constraint that is not 2-monotone. Then $\{f_0, f_1, f_2\}$ can strictly implement the function* XOR.

Proof: If either f_0 or f_1 is C-closed, then Lemma 5.24 gives us a strict implementation of the XOR function. Otherwise, using Lemma 5.24, we can strictly implement the functions F and T. Now the lemma follows from an application of Lemma 5.36. $\square$

5.4.10   Miscellaneous

Definition 5.38 *A family $\mathcal{F}'$ is said to be a basis for a family $\mathcal{F}$ if every constraint in $\mathcal{F}$ can be expressed as a conjunction of constraints in $\mathcal{F}'$.*

Example 5.39 *The family $\{T, F, OR_0, OR_1, OR_2\}$ is a basis for the family of bijunctive constraints.*

Proposition 5.40 *If $\mathcal{F}'$ is a basis of $\mathcal{F}$, then $\mathcal{F}'$ perfectly (but not necessarily strictly or faithfully) implements every constraint in $\mathcal{F}$.*

Proof: Let $f \in \mathcal{F}$ be given by $f(x) = f_1(x) \wedge \cdots \wedge f_l(x)$, where $f_1, \ldots, f_l \in \mathcal{F}'$. Then the constraints $f_1(x), f_2(x), \ldots, f_l(x)$ give a perfect l implementation of f. $\square$

Let us introduce a new constraint $SymOR_1$:

$$SymOR_1(x, y, z) \equiv (F(x) \wedge OR_1(y, z)) \vee (T(x) \wedge OR_1(z, y)).$$

Lemma 5.41 *Let $\mathcal{F}$ be a set of 0-valid constraints. Suppose that $\mathcal{F}$ contains a function f_+ which is not weakly positive, a function f_- which is not weakly negative and a function g which is not affine. If every constraint in $\mathcal{F}$ is C-closed, then $\mathcal{F}$ can perfectly implement $SymOR_1$. Otherwise $\mathcal{F}$ can perfectly implement OR_1.*

Proof: Let us first prove that $\{f_+, f_-, g, F\}$ can perfectly implement OR_1. According to the characterization of affine 0-valid functions (see Lemma 4.10), there are two assignments s_1 and s_2 such that $g(s_1) = g(s_2) = 1$ but $g(s_1 \oplus s_2 \oplus \vec{0}) = g(s_1 \oplus s_2) = 0$. The following table describes the situation:

					$g()$
	00...0	00...0	00...0	00...0	1
s_1	00...0	00...0	11...1	11...1	1
s_2	00...0	11...1	00...0	11...1	1
$s_1 \oplus s_2$	00...0	11...1	11...1	00...0	0
	00...0	$xx...x$	$yy...y$	$zz...z$	

Fixing the above variables to 0's as shown in the last row, and assigning replicated copies of three variables x, y and z, we get a constraint $h_0(x, y, z)$, such that $h_0(000) = h_0(011) = h_0(101) = 1$ and $h_0(110) = 0$. (Notice that forcing variables to 0 is feasible since the constraint F is available.)

Following the characterization of weakly negative functions (see Lemma 4.8), there are two assignments s_1' and s_2' such that $f_-(s_1') = f_-(s_2') = 1$ but $f_-(s_1' \cap s_2') = 0$. The following table describes the situation:

					$f_-()$
	00...0	00...0	00...0	00...0	1
s_1	00...0	00...0	11...1	11...1	1
s_2	00...0	11...1	00...0	11...1	1
$s_1 \cap s_2$	00...0	00...0	00...0	11...1	0
	00...0	$xx...x$	$yy...y$	$zz...z$	

Fixing the above variables to 0's as shown in the last row, and assigning replicated copies of three variables x, y and z, we get a constraint $h_0'(x, y, z)$, such that $h_0'(0,0,0) = h_0'(0,1,1) = h_0'(1,0,1) = 1$ and $h_0'(0,0,1) = 0$.

In using a similar characterization of weakly positive constraints, we can perfectly implement a constraint $h_0''(x, y, z)$ obtained from f_+ such that $h_0''(0,0,0) = h_0''(0,1,1) = h_0''(1,0,1) = 1$ but $h_0''(1,1,1) = 0$.

Now let us denote by $k_0(x, y, z)$ the following conjunction of constraint applications:

$$h_0(x, y, z) \wedge h_0'(x, y, z) \wedge h_0''(x, y, z).$$

To conclude, there are several cases we need to analyze.

- If $k_0(0, 1, 0) = 1$, then $\{h_0(x, y, z), h_0'(x, y, z), h_0''(x, y, z), \mathsf{F}(x)\}$ is a perfect implementation of $y \vee \bar{z}$,

- If $k_0(0, 1, 0) = 0$, then $\{h_0(x, y, z), h_0'(x, y, z), h_0''(x, y, z)\}$ is a perfect implementation of $\bar{y} \vee z$, with x as an auxiliary variable.

This proves that $\{f_+, f_-, g, \mathsf{F}\}$ can perfectly implement OR_1.

If there is a constraint h in $\mathcal{F}$ which is not C-closed, since h is 0-valid, h can perfectly implement either the function OR_1 or F (see Lemma 5.25). In both cases $\mathcal{F}$ can perfectly implement (directly or by composition) the function OR_1. Otherwise, let us consider the set of $\{f_+, f_-, g, \mathsf{F}\}$-constraint applications that implements OR_1. Use x_0 in place of any variable with the constraint $\mathsf{F}(y)$. In using the C-closed property of every constraint, it is easy to see that this set of constraint applications perfectly implements the function SymOR_1. $\qquad\square$

Chapter 6

Classification Theorems for Decision, Counting and Quantified Problems

We now study the complexity of the decision, counting and quantified variants of the constraint satisfaction problems. We will show that each of these classes exhibits a dichotomy — any problem in each of these classes is either "easy" or at least as "hard" as any other problem in the corresponding class. Such dichotomy results are a rare phenomenon in the study of complexity theory. Our proof techniques build on the results of the preceding chapter; we will show that our implementation lemmas give simple proofs for these dichotomy theorems. While the dichotomy result for the decision and counting problems were previously known, the dichotomy result for the quantified constraint satisfaction problems is new.

6.1 Preliminaries

To reduce a problem $\mathsf{SAT}(\mathcal{F})$ ($\#\mathsf{SAT}(\mathcal{F})$) to a problem $\mathsf{SAT}(\mathcal{F}')$ ($\#\mathsf{SAT}(\mathcal{F}')$), we will often use $\mathsf{SAT}(\mathcal{F}' \cup \{\mathsf{F}, \mathsf{T}\})$ ($\#\mathsf{SAT}(\mathcal{F}' \cup \{\mathsf{F}, \mathsf{T}\})$) as an intermediate problem. We will show that for our purposes, the functions F and T can be easily implemented, provided the family $\mathcal{F}'$ is not C-closed. However, it is not possible to do so when the family $\mathcal{F}'$ is C-closed. In this particular case we will use the following lemma.

Lemma 6.1 *Let $\mathcal{F}$ be a set of C-closed constraints. If $\mathsf{SAT}(\mathcal{F} \cup \{\mathsf{F}, \mathsf{T}\})$ is NP-hard (P-hard) and if $\mathcal{F}$ can perfectly implement the XOR function, then $\mathsf{SAT}(\mathcal{F})$ is NP-hard (P-hard). If $\#\mathsf{SAT}(\mathcal{F} \cup \{\mathsf{F}, \mathsf{T}\})$) is #P-hard and if $\mathcal{F}$ can faithfully implement the XOR function, then $\#\mathsf{SAT}(\mathcal{F})$ is #P-hard.*

Proof: First we show a log-space (counting) reduction from $\mathsf{SAT}(\mathcal{F} \cup \{\mathsf{F}, \mathsf{T}\})$ ($\#\mathsf{SAT}(\mathcal{F} \cup \{\mathsf{F}, \mathsf{T}\})$) to $\mathsf{SAT}(\mathcal{F} \cup \{\mathsf{XOR}\})$ ($\#\mathsf{SAT}(\mathcal{F} \cup \{\mathsf{XOR}\})$). It suffices to use two new variables, x_0 and x_1, that will simulate the role of functions F and T. Let $\mathcal{C}$ be an $\mathcal{F} \cup \{\mathsf{F}, \mathsf{T}\}$-collection of constraint applications on variables $\vec{x}$. We use the variable x_0 in place of any variable y with the constraint $\mathsf{F}(y)$ and the variable x_1 in place of any variable z with the constraint $\mathsf{T}(z)$. Next we add the constraint $\mathsf{XOR}(x_0, x_1)$. We get $\mathcal{C}'$, an $\mathcal{F} \cup \{\mathsf{XOR}\}$-collection of constraint applications on variables $\vec{x}, x_0, x_1$. Let s be an assignment to $\vec{x}$ that satisfies all constraints in $\mathcal{C}$. Extending s by $s(x_0) = 0$ and $s(x_1) = 1$ yields a satisfying assignment for $\mathcal{C}'$. Conversely, let s' be an assignment to $\vec{x} \cup x_0 \cup x_1$ that satisfies all constraints in $\mathcal{C}'$. If $s'(x_0) = 0$ and $s'(x_1) = 1$, then s' restricted to $\vec{x}$ satisfies $\mathcal{C}$. Otherwise, $s'(x_0) = 1$ and $s'(x_1) = 0$. Then, in using the C-closed property of every function in $\mathcal{F}$ it is easy to verify that the assignment $s(x) = 1 - s'(x)$ satisfies all constraints in $\mathcal{C}$. At this stage we can conclude that $\mathsf{SAT}(\mathcal{F} \cup \{\mathsf{XOR}\})$ is NP-hard (P-hard). Moreover, the number of satisfying assignments for $\mathcal{C}'$ is twice the number of satisfying assignments for $\mathcal{C}$. Hence the proposed reduction is a counting reduction, thus proving the #P-hardness of $\#\mathsf{SAT}(\mathcal{F} \cup \{\mathsf{XOR}\})$. Finally, if $\mathcal{F}$ can perfectly (faithfully) implement the XOR function then we can conclude by using Lemma 5.12 (Lemma 5.15). $\square$

6.2   The class SAT

Decision version of our constraint satisfaction problems were studied by Schaefer [82]. Schaefer referred to these problems as the *generalized satisfiability problems* and he showed the following dichotomy theorem: each satisfiability problem is either in P or is NP-complete. Moreover, he identified a concise characterization that separates the easy problems from the hard ones.

Theorem 6.2 [82] *Given a constraint set $\mathcal{F}$, the problem $\mathsf{SAT}(\mathcal{F})$ is in P if $\mathcal{F}$ satisfies one of the conditions below, and $\mathsf{SAT}(\mathcal{F})$ is otherwise NP-complete.*

1. *$\mathcal{F}$ is 0-valid (1-valid).*

2. *$\mathcal{F}$ is weakly positive (weakly negative).*

3. *$\mathcal{F}$ is affine.*

4. *$\mathcal{F}$ is bijunctive.*

We now establish Schaefer's result. Our proof relies on the following key lemma.

Lemma 6.3 [hardness lemma for satisfiability] *Let $\mathcal{F}$ be any collection of constraints that contains:*

- *a constraint $f_+ \in \mathcal{F}$ such that f_+ is not weakly positive.*

- *a constraint $f_- \in \mathcal{F}$ such that f_- is not weakly negative.*

- *a constraint f_a such that f_a is not affine.*

- *a constraint f_b such that f_b is not bijunctive.*

Then $\mathcal{F} \cup \{\mathsf{F}, \mathsf{T}\}$ can perfectly implement the constraint $\mathsf{One\_in\_Three}$.

Proof: We first use the family $\{f_+, f_-, \mathsf{F}, \mathsf{T}\}$ to perfectly implement the XOR function (Lemma 5.26) and the family $\{f_a, \mathsf{F}\}$ to perfectly implement one of the functions OR_0, OR_1 or OR_2 (Lemma 5.30). By Lemma 5.32, we know that the family $\{\mathsf{OR}_i, \mathsf{XOR}\}$ for any $i \in \{0, 1, 2\}$ can perfectly implement each of the functions OR_0, OR_1 and OR_2. Finally, we use family $\{f_b, \mathsf{OR}_0, \mathsf{OR}_1, \mathsf{OR}_2\}$ to perfectly implement the function $\mathsf{One\_in\_Three}$ (Lemma 5.33). $\square$

Lemma 6.4 [82] SAT({One_in_Three}) *is* NP-*hard.*

Proof: See Example 5.13.   □

Proof of Theorem 6.2: The SAT($\mathcal{F}$) problem is easily seen to be in NP. The polynomial
time solvable cases are classical. If every constraint is 0-valid (1-valid), then every set of
constraint applications is completely satisfiable by the trivial all false (true) assignment. If
every constraint is weakly negative, then every set of constraint applications can be seen as
a Horn formula, whose satisfiability can be decided in linear time (see [25] and [71]) (the
case weakly positive can be treated similarly). If every constraint is bijunctive, then every
set of constraint applications can be seen as a 2CNF formula, whose satisfiability can be
decided in linear time (see [5]). If every constraint is affine, then every set of constraint
applications can be seen as a linear system of equations over the finite field GF(2). Thus
its satisfiability can be decided in polynomial time using Gaussian elimination.

On the other hand, suppose that $\mathcal{F}$ does not satisfy any of the above conditions. Then
$\mathcal{F} \cup \{\mathsf{F}, \mathsf{T}\}$ perfectly implements the NP-hard constraint One_in_Three (Lemma 6.3 and
Lemma 6.4). Therefore, by Lemma 5.12 SAT($\mathcal{F} \cup \{\mathsf{F}, \mathsf{T}\}$) is NP-hard. Now if $\mathcal{F}$ contains
a function h which is not C-closed, we can perfectly implement the functions F and T
(Lemma 5.24). Using Lemma 5.12 we get NP-hardness for SAT($\mathcal{F}$) in this case. Otherwise,
$\mathcal{F}$ is C-closed. By Lemma 5.24, we can perfectly implement the XOR function and conclude
the NP-hardness result by using Lemma 6.1.   □

This complexity classification can be refined in terms of parallel computation. The following theorem characterizes the parallel complexity of finding a satisfying truth assigment
of an $\mathcal{F}$-collection of constraint applications for every constraint set $\mathcal{F}$ such that the problem
SAT($\mathcal{F}$) is in P.

Theorem 6.5 *Let $\mathcal{F}$ be a constraint set such that* SAT($\mathcal{F}$) *is in* P. *If $\mathcal{F}$ satisfies one of
the following conditions, then* SAT($\mathcal{F}$) *is in* NC; *otherwise,* SAT($\mathcal{F}$) *is* P-*complete.*

1. $\mathcal{F}$ *is 0-valid (resp., 1-valid).*

2. $\mathcal{F}$ *is affine.*

3. $\mathcal{F}$ *is bijunctive.*

4. $\mathcal{F}$ *is IHS-B+(resp., IHS-B−).*

Proof: If every constraint in $\mathcal{F}$ is 0-valid (resp., 1-Valid), then the all-zero (resp., all-one)
assignment trivially satisfies any $\mathcal{F}$-collection of constraint applications.

If every constraint in $\mathcal{F}$ is bijunctive then the problem of finding a satisfying assignment
to an $\mathcal{F}$-collection of constraint applications is in AC^1 [16], a subclass of NC^2.

If every constraint in $\mathcal{F}$ is affine then this problem is equivalent to find a solution of a
linear system over the field $GF(2)$. Therefore, it is in NC^2 [73].

Finally, suppose that every constraint in $\mathcal{F}$ is IHS-B+(it is similar if every relation is
IHS-B−). An $\mathcal{F}$-collection of constraint applications can be seen as a set $\mathcal{C}$ of clauses,
$\mathcal{C} = \mathcal{P} \cup \mathcal{B}$ where $\mathcal{P}$ is a set of positive clauses and $\mathcal{B}$ a set of clauses either of the form $(\bar{x})$
or $(\bar{x} \vee y)$. One can use an algorithm similar in spirit to the one proposed by Cook and
Luby [16]. A high level description of this algorithm is as follows.

- From the set of clauses $\mathcal{B}$, defined over a set of n variables, construct a digraph $G = (V, E)$. There is a vertex in V for each of the $2n$ literals. The edges E are formed from the clauses as follows. For each clause $(\bar{x})$ in $\mathcal{B}$ we add to E the directed edge $x \to \bar{x}$, for each clause $(\bar{x} \vee y)$ in $\mathcal{B}$ we add to E two directed edges $x \to y$ and $\bar{y} \to \bar{x}$. (Observe that G is acyclic for the set of clauses $\mathcal{B}$ is trivially satisfiable).

- Let A be the adjacency matrix for G; i.e., the rows and columns of A are indexed by the literals and an entry in A is 1 if it corresponds to an edge in E and it is 0 otherwise, with the exception that each diagonal entry in A is 1.

- Let A' be the matrix A raised to the power $2n$ using the operations $(\vee, \wedge)$ in place of $(+, .)$. There is a path from literal l to literal l' in G if and only if $A'_{ll'} = 1$.

- Let F_0 be the set of variables x such that $(\bar{x})$ is a clause in $\mathcal{B}$. For each x in F_0 set $s_0(x) = 0$.

- For each variable y, if there is an x_0 in F_0 such that $A'_{\bar{x}_0 \bar{y}} = 1$, then set $s_0(y) = 0$; otherwise, set $s_0(y) = 1$

  In this way one gets the generic assignment, s_0, for $\mathcal{B}$: $s_0 = \bigcup_{s \in \text{SAT}(\mathcal{B})} s$.

- Verify that s_0 satisfies $\mathcal{P}$.

It is easy to see that $\mathcal{C}$ is satisfiable if and only if s_0 satisfies $\mathcal{P}$. The resources required by the algorithm are dominated by the computation of A' (which can be done by squaring A $\log(2n)$ times using the operations $(\vee, \wedge)$). Hence, this problem is also in NC, thus completing the proof of the NC case of Theorem 6.5.

The P-complete case was stated by Schaefer [82, Theorem 5.1, L3, page 224]. We will use the following P-completeness result:

Proposition 6.6 [50] (see also [36, A.6.3, page 168]) $\text{SAT}(\{\text{OR}_{3,2}, \mathsf{F}, \mathsf{T}\})$ *and* $\text{SAT}(\{\text{OR}_{3,1}, \mathsf{F}, \mathsf{T}\})$ *are P-complete.*

Let $\mathcal{F}$ be a constraint set such that $\text{SAT}(\mathcal{F})$ is in P and such that $\mathcal{F}$ does not satisfy any condition of the theorem. According to Theorem 6.2 every constraint in $\mathcal{F}$ is weakly negative (weakly positive) but at least one of these functions is not IHS-$B-$(IHS-$B+$). Hence, $\mathcal{F} \cup \{\mathsf{F}, \mathsf{T}\}$ perfectly implements the constraint $\text{OR}_{3,2}$ ($\text{OR}_{3,1}$); see Lemma 5.27. Therefore, by Proposition 6.6 and Lemma 5.14, $\text{SAT}(\mathcal{F} \cup \{\mathsf{F}, \mathsf{T}\})$ is P-hard.

Now, since $\mathcal{F}$ contains at least one non-0-valid constraint and one non-1-valid constraint, $\mathcal{F}$ can perfectly implement either F and T, or XOR depending on whether $\mathcal{F}$ is C-closed (Lemmas 5.24 and 5.25). In either case, we conclude the P-hardness result by using Lemma 5.14 or Lemma 6.1. $\square$

6.3   The class #SAT

The counting version of our constraint satisfaction problems were studied by Creignou and Hermann [19]. As with Schaefer, they obtained a dichotomy theorem (FP/ #P-complete) and identified a concise characterization that separates the easy counting problems from the hard ones.

Theorem 6.7 [19] *Given a constraint set $\mathcal{F}$, the problem $\#\text{SAT}(\mathcal{F})$ is in FP if $\mathcal{F}$ is an affine family of constraints, and it is otherwise #P-complete.*

The proof of this theorem relies on the following #P-completeness results.

Lemma 6.8 [89, 78, 67]. $\#\mathsf{SAT}(\{\mathsf{OR}_0\})$, $\#\mathsf{SAT}(\{\mathsf{OR}_2\})$ and $\#\mathsf{SAT}(\{\mathsf{OR}_1\})$ are #P-complete.

Proof of Theorem 6.7: The $\#\mathsf{SAT}(\mathcal{F})$ problem is easily seen to be in #P. If every constraint in $\mathcal{F}$ is affine, then an instance of $\#\mathsf{SAT}(\mathcal{F})$ can be viewed as a system of linear equations over $\mathrm{GF}(2)$. We can use Gaussian elimination to determine the number of satisfying solutions in polynomial time.

On the other hand, suppose that $\mathcal{F}$ contains a function g which is not affine. We will show that the problem $\#\mathsf{SAT}(\mathcal{F})$ is #P-hard. There are three cases to distinguish.

g is neither 0-valid nor 1-valid: In this case, the family $\{g, \mathsf{F}, \mathsf{T}\}$ can faithfully implement one of the functions OR_0, OR_1 or OR_2 (Lemma 5.30). Hence, by Lemma 5.15 and Lemma 6.8, $\#\mathsf{SAT}(\mathcal{F} \cup \{\mathsf{F}, \mathsf{T}\})$ is #P-hard.

Now if $\mathcal{F}$ contains a function h which is not C-closed, we can faithfully implement the functions F and T (Lemma 5.24); hence, using Lemma 5.15, we get #P-hardness for $\#\mathsf{SAT}(\mathcal{F})$ in this case. Otherwise, $\mathcal{F}$ is C-closed. By Lemma 5.24 we can faithfully implement the XOR function and conclude the #P-hardness result by using Lemma 6.1.

g is 0-valid but is not 1-valid (or vice versa): In this case, $\{g, F\}$ can faithfully implement one of the functions OR_1 or OR_2 (Lemma 5.30). Also, it is clear that $\{g\}$ can faithfully implement F since g is 0-valid and not 1-valid. Thus $\mathcal{F}$ can faithfully implement one of the functions OR_1 or OR_2. Using Lemma 5.15 and Lemma 6.8 we get #P-hardness for $\#\mathsf{SAT}(\mathcal{F})$ in this case.

g is 0-valid and 1-valid: If g is not C-closed, then $\{g\}$ can faithfully implement the function OR_1 (Lemma 5.25). Otherwise, the family $\{g, F\}$ can faithfully implement one of the functions OR_1, or OR_2 (Lemma 5.30). Now, using as before the C-closed property of g, it is easy to see that this implies the existence of a counting reduction from $\#\mathsf{SAT}(\mathsf{OR}_1)$ or $\#\mathsf{SAT}(\mathsf{OR}_2)$ to $\#\mathsf{SAT}(\{g\})$, thus establishing the #P-hardness for $\#\mathsf{SAT}(\mathcal{F})$. $\square$

It is interesting to compare the results of the two previous theorems. Now we know exactly what are the polynomial-time solvable satisfiability problems whose counting counterparts are #P-complete and we get that the NP-completeness of a satisfiability decision problem implies the #P-completeness of the corresponding counting problem.

Another closely related aspect of interest is that of enumerating all the solutions. Generating all configurations that satisfy a given specification is a well-studied problem in combinatorics. In practice, the enumeration problem may arise quite naturally; for instance, when there exist some additional complex conditions that are too difficult to be incorporated directly into the constraints problem.

A *generating algorithm* is an algorithm that generates all configurations that satisfy a given specification (e.g., all satisfying truth assignments of a given formula) without duplicate. One has to be careful in defining the notion of polynomial time for such algorithms. Indeed, in most interesting problems the number of configurations to be generated is potentially exponential in the size of the input. For this reason Johnson, Yannakakis and Papadimitriou [47] defined *polynomial-delay algorithms*.

Definition 6.9 [generating algorithm with polynomial delay] [47] *A generating algorithm has polynomial delay if it generates the configurations, one after the other, in such a way* *that the delay until the first is output, and thereafter the delay between any two consecutive configurations (and between the last configuration and the halting) is bounded by a polynomial in the input size.*

Creignou and Hébrard [18] refined Schaefer's result in identifying satisfiability problems for which all the solutions can be generated with polynomial delay.

Theorem 6.10 [18] *Given a constraint set $\mathcal{F}$, the problem of generating all models for any given $\mathcal{F}$-collection of constraints has a polynomial space, polynomial delay algorithm if $\mathcal{F}$ satisfies one of the conditions below, and otherwise, no such algorithm exists unless* P = NP.

1. *$\mathcal{F}$ is weakly positive (weakly negative).*

2. *$\mathcal{F}$ is affine.*

3. *$\mathcal{F}$ is bijunctive.*

Proof: Observe that if $\mathcal{F}$ satisfies one of the three conditions above then $\mathcal{F} \cup \{F, T\}$ still satisfies this condition and thus $\mathsf{SAT}(\mathcal{F} \cup \{F, T\})$ is in P by Theorem 6.2. We can then conclude that there is a simple recursive algorithm which enumerates all models of a given $\mathcal{F}$-collection of constraint applications (see [89, Fact 7]).

Otherwise, denote by $\mathsf{SAT}^*(\mathcal{F})$ the variant of $\mathsf{SAT}(\mathcal{F})$ in which the objective is to find a non-trivial satisfying Boolean assignment, i.e. an assignment that is different from $\vec{0}$ and $\vec{1}$. The following proposition entails that there are satisfiability problems for which even though one satisfying solution can be found trivially, the problem of finding a second one is NP-hard.

Proposition 6.11 *Let $\mathcal{F}$ be a constraint set. If $\mathcal{F}$ contains a constraint f_+ which is not weakly positive, a constraint f_- which is not weakly negative, a constraint f_a which is not affine, a constraint f_b which is not bijunctive, then $\mathsf{SAT}^*(\mathcal{F})$ is NP-hard.*

This proposition clearly completes the proof of Theorem 6.10.   □

Proof of Proposition 6.11: First observe that if $\mathcal{F}$ contains a constraint f_0 which is not 0-valid and a constraint f_1 which is not 1-valid, then by Theorem 6.2, $\mathsf{SAT}(\mathcal{F})$ is NP-hard; and hence, $\mathsf{SAT}^*(\mathcal{F})$ is NP-hard as well.

Now suppose that every function in $\mathcal{F}$ is 0-valid (the case 1-valid can be treated similarly). In this case finding a first solution is trivial. According to Theorem 6.2, $\mathsf{SAT}(\mathcal{F} \cup \{F, T\})$ is NP-hard. Our proof consists of a reduction from $\mathsf{SAT}(\mathcal{F} \cup \{F, T\})$ to $\mathsf{SAT}^*(\mathcal{F})$. We transform any $(\mathcal{F} \cup \{F, T\})$-collection of constraint applications $\mathcal{C}$ to an $\mathcal{F}$-collection of constraint applications $\mathcal{C}'$ such that $\mathcal{C}'$ has a non-trivial satisfying assignment if and only if $\mathcal{C}$ is satisfiable. The main tool is Lemma 5.41 which shows that $\mathcal{F}$ can perfectly implement either OR_1 or SymOR_1. To do this transformation, we replace in $\mathcal{C}$ any variable y that appears in a constraint $F(y)$ by a variable x_0, and any variable z that appears in a constraint $T(z)$ by a variable x_1. We now delete all constraint applications of the functions F and T. Next, using Lemma 5.41, we add either the constraints $\mathsf{OR}_1(x_0, x_1)$, $\mathsf{OR}_1(x_0, x)$ and $\mathsf{OR}_1(x, x_1)$, or the constraints $\mathsf{SymOR}_1(x_0, x_1)$, $\mathsf{SymOR}_1(x_0, x)$ and $\mathsf{SymOR}_1(x, x_1)$ for every variable x. It is easy to verify that there exists a satisfying Boolean assignment for $\mathcal{C}$ if and only if there exists a satisfying Boolean assignment different from $\vec{0}$ and $\vec{1}$ for $\mathcal{C}'$, thus proving the NP-hardness of $\mathsf{SAT}^*(\mathcal{F})$.   □

6.4 The class QSAT

There is also a dichotomy result for quantified constraint satisfaction problems. Dalmau has independently observed such a result [23]. For the hard case the proof technique is similar to the one used for the above theorems. However, the polynomial-time solvable cases are less classical.

Theorem 6.12 *Let $\mathcal{F}$ be a constraint set. If $\mathcal{F}$ satisfies one of the following three conditions, then* QSAT$(\mathcal{F})$ *is in* P *otherwise it is* PSPACE-*complete.*

1. *$\mathcal{F}$ is weakly positive (weakly negative).*

2. *$\mathcal{F}$ is affine.*

3. *$\mathcal{F}$ is bijunctive.*

Proof: First note that the problem QSAT$(\mathcal{F})$ is in PSPACE. We can check whether a set of quantified $\mathcal{F}$-expression is true by cycling through all possible assignments for the variables $x_1, \ldots x_n$ and evaluating the constraints for each. Recording the current assignment, testing the truth value of the set of constraint applications and keeping track of where we are in the process can all be done in polynomial space.

If every constraint in $\mathcal{F}$ is weakly positive (weakly negative) or if every constraint in $\mathcal{F}$ is bijunctive, then the problem QSAT$(\mathcal{F})$ is known to be in P (see [60] and [5], resp.). If every constraint in $\mathcal{F}$ is affine, then an $\mathcal{F}$-expression can be seen as a quantified linear system over $GF(2)$. In using Gaussian elimination (thus in polynomial time) one can either show that this system has no solution or transform it into an equivalent triangular linear system $S = \{E_1, \ldots, E_p\}$ over a set of variables $X = \{x_1, \ldots, x_n\}$ in which $p \leq n$ and E_i only involves variables in $\{x_i, \ldots, x_n\}$ for $i \leq n$. In the first case we are done and the initial quantified $\mathcal{F}$-expression is false. Otherwise, it suffices to call the following function, which decides whether a quantified triangular system of linear equations over $GF(2)$ is evaluated to be true.

> Function Eval $(Q_1 x_1 \ldots Q_n x_n, S)$
> If $S = \emptyset$, then return(True)
> Else if x_n does not occur in any equation of S,
>   then return(Eval($Q_1 x_1 \ldots Q_{n-1} x_{n-1}, S$))
>   else if $Q_n = \forall$, then return(False)
>   else let j_0 be the greatest j such that x_n occurs in E_j,
>   using E_{j_0} express x_n as a function of $x_{j_0}, \ldots x_{n-1}$,
>   in S replace x_n by this function in any other equation,
>   return(Eval($Q_1 x_1 \ldots Q_{n-1} x_{n-1}, S \setminus E_{j_0}$))

This algorithm can clearly be performed in polynomial time, thus proving that if every constraint in $\mathcal{F}$ is affine then QSAT$(\mathcal{F})$ is in P.

Conversely, if $\mathcal{F}$ does not satisfy any of the conditions of the theorem, we will show that QSAT$(\mathcal{F})$ is PSPACE-hard using the following proposition.

Proposition 6.13 QSAT$(\{$One_in_Three$\})$ *is* PSPACE-*hard.*

Proof: Q3SAT is known to be PSPACE-complete [85], [86], and we know that the constraint One_in_Three can perfectly implement any ternary function (see Lemma 5.13). Therefore, by Lemma 5.16, we get that QSAT$(\{$One_in_Three$\})$ is PSPACE-hard.   □

Suppose that $\mathcal{F}$ does not satisfy any of the conditions of the theorem. Then $\mathcal{F} \cup \{\mathsf{F}, \mathsf{T}\}$ can implement with perfect completeness the function $\mathsf{One\_in\_Three}$ (see Lemma 6.3). Thus by Lemma 5.16 and Proposition 6.13, we get that $\mathsf{QSAT}(\mathcal{F} \cup \{\mathsf{T}, \mathsf{F}\})$ is PSPACE-hard.

Now it remains to eliminate the functions F and T. The proof can be handled in much the same way as the proof of Proposition 6.11. Once again we have at our disposal either the constraint OR_1 or SymOR_1 (Lemma 5.41). We will transform a quantified $(\mathcal{F} \cup \{\mathsf{F}, \mathsf{T}\})$-expression to a quantified $\mathcal{F}$-expression. Suppose that the initial instance is of the form $\mathcal{Q}_2 x_2 \ldots \mathcal{Q}_n x_n \mathcal{C}$. We use a new variable x_0 in place of each variable y that appears in a constraint $\mathsf{F}(y)$ and a new variable x_1 in place of each variable z that appears in a constraint $\mathsf{T}(z)$. We now delete all constraint applications of the functions F and T and let $\mathcal{C}'$ be the resulting collection of constraint applications. We also introduce a variable x. Next we consider either the following expression:

$$\exists x_0 \exists x_1 \forall x \mathcal{Q}_2 x_2 \ldots \mathcal{Q}_n x_n \quad \mathcal{C}' \cup \{\mathsf{OR}_1(x_0, x_1), \mathsf{OR}_1(x_0, x), \mathsf{OR}_1(x, x_1)\} \text{ or,}$$

$$\exists x_0 \exists x_1 \forall x \mathcal{Q}_2 x_2 \ldots \mathcal{Q}_n x_n \quad \mathcal{C}' \cup \{\mathsf{SymOR}_1(x_0, x_1), \mathsf{SymOR}_1(x_0, x), \mathsf{SymOR}_1(x, x_1)\}.$$

It is easy to verify that this quantified $\mathcal{F}$-expression is true if and only if the initial quantified $(\mathcal{F} \cup \{\mathsf{F}, \mathsf{T}\})$-expression is true. Hence, $\mathsf{QSAT}(\mathcal{F} \cup \{\mathsf{F}, \mathsf{T}\})$ is log-space reducible to $\mathsf{QSAT}(\mathcal{F})$, thus completing the proof of Theorem 6.12. $\square$

Chapter 7

Classification Theorems for Optimization Problems

Recall that in Chapter 3, we associated four basic variants of optimization problems with any constraint family. Their goals were:

1. Finding an assignment that maximizes the number of satisfied constraints.

2. Finding an assignment with the maximum number of variables set to 1 that satisfies all given constraints.

3. Finding an assignment that minimizes the number of unsatisfied constraints.

4. Finding an assignment with minimum number of variables set to 1 that satisfies all given constraints.

In this section we study each of the above category of optimization problems and classify them. At first glance, this appears to be redundant work. For instance, task (1) and (3) above seem to be restatements of the same problems! It turns out, however, that the natural correspondence between the two problems only preserves optimality, but not approximability! Our classification reveals many differences between the approximability behavior of maximization and minimization problems.

In our study of the above classes of problems, we will consider unweighted as well as weighted versions of these problems. In all cases, the algorithmic results apply to the weighted version of problems while the inapproximability results hold for the unweighted versions. We will stress this fact in the individual lemmas by stating positive results for weighted problems and (the final) negative results for unweighted problems.

We remark that the literature on constraint satisfaction problems includes one more class of optimization problems. Reith and Vollmer [80] study the problem of finding the lexicographically smallest assignment satisfying an $\mathcal{F}$-collection of constraint applications. They get a dichotomy classification of the problems in this class as polynomial time solvable or OptP-complete (where OptP is a class of optimization problems defined in [62]). We will not be covering this family of results in our study here.

7.1   Weighted versus unweighted optimization problems

We start by examining the relationship between the weighted and unweighted versions of the optimization problems considered in this chapter. We first prove a result of [22, Theorem 4] which reduces the impact of the weights in weighted optimization problems. The proof is a special case of a general technique known as scaling.

Lemma 7.1 *For every $\mathcal{F}$ such that* Weighted MAX SAT$(\mathcal{F})$ *is in* poly-APX, Weighted MAX SAT$(\mathcal{F})$ *AP-reduces to the special class of* Weighted MAX SAT$(\mathcal{F})$ *problems with polynomially bounded positive integral weights. Analogous results hold for* Weighted MIN SAT$(\mathcal{F})$, Weighted MAX ONES$(\mathcal{F})$ *and* Weighted MIN ONES$(\mathcal{F})$.

Proof: Given an instance $\mathcal{I}$ of, say, Weighted MAX SAT$(\mathcal{F})$, with weights $w_1, \ldots, w_m$, we first compute an approximation A to the value of the optimum of $\mathcal{I}$. Since the problem is assumed to be in poly-APX, we know $A \leq \mathrm{OPT}(\mathcal{I}) \leq p(m)A$, for some polynomial $p(\cdot)$. We now create an instance $\mathcal{I}'$ of Weighted MAX SAT$(\mathcal{F})$ that has the same variables and constraint applications as $\mathcal{I}$ but with integers weights $w_1', \ldots, w_m'$ chosen as follows. Let $M = m^2 p(m)$ be an integer. Set $w_j' = \lfloor \frac{M w_j}{A} \rfloor + 1$.

Given an r-approximate solution s to $\mathcal{I}'$, we output either the solution given by the $p(m)$ approximation algorithm to $\mathcal{I}$ or the solution s, whichever is better. We claim such a solution is an $r(1 + \frac{4}{m})$-approximate solution to $\mathcal{I}$ provided $m \geq 4$, which satisfies the condition of the AP-reduction that the solution be $1 + c(r - 1) + o(1)$-approximate, where the $o(1)$ is with respect to m.

The claim is obvious if $r > p(m)$; so we assume $r \leq p(m)$. Notice that the optimum of $\mathcal{I}'$ has value at least $\frac{M}{A}\mathrm{OPT}(\mathcal{I})$. Thus s achieves an objective value of at least $\frac{M}{rA}\mathrm{OPT}(\mathcal{I})$ as a solution to $\mathcal{I}'$. Hence as a solution to $\mathcal{I}$ it achieves an objective of at least

$$
\begin{aligned}
\frac{A}{M}\left(\frac{M}{rA}\mathrm{OPT}(\mathcal{I}) - 2m\right) &= \frac{\mathrm{OPT}(\mathcal{I})}{r} - \frac{2mA}{M} \\
&= \frac{\mathrm{OPT}(\mathcal{I})}{r} - \frac{2mA}{m^2 p(m)} \\
&\geq \frac{\mathrm{OPT}(\mathcal{I})}{r} - \frac{2m\mathrm{OPT}(\mathcal{I})}{m^2 p(m)} \\
&= \frac{\mathrm{OPT}(\mathcal{I})}{r}\left(1 - \frac{2r}{mp(m)}\right) \\
&\geq \frac{\mathrm{OPT}(\mathcal{I})}{r}\left(1 - \frac{2}{m}\right) \\
&\geq \frac{\mathrm{OPT}(\mathcal{I})}{r}\frac{1}{\left(1 + \frac{4}{m}\right)}
\end{aligned}
$$

(where the last inequality uses $m \geq 4$). Thus the reduction satisfies the requirements of an AP-reduction. $\square$

Lemma 7.2 *For any constraint family $\mathcal{F}$, if* Weighted MAX SAT$(\mathcal{F})$ *is in* poly-APX, *then* Weighted MAX SAT$(\mathcal{F})$*AP-reduces to* MAX SAT$(\mathcal{F})$. *Analogous results hold for* MIN SAT$(\mathcal{F})$, MAX ONES$(\mathcal{F})$ *and* MIN ONES$(\mathcal{F})$.

Proof: We first use Lemma 7.1 to assume that the weights are polynomially bounded positive integers. We then remove the integer weights by replication of constraints/variables, depending on the category of the optimization problem, as described below.

Given an instance of Weighted MAX SAT$(\mathcal{F})$ on variables $x_1, \ldots, x_n$, constraints $C_1, \ldots, C_m$ and weights $w_1, \ldots, w_m$, we reduce it to the unweighted case by replication of constraints. Thus the reduced instance has variables $x_1, \ldots, x_n$ and constraint $\{\{C_i^j\}_{j=1}^{w_i}\}_{i=1}^m$, where constraint $C_i^j = C_i$. It is clear that the reduced instance is essentially the same as the instance we started with. Similarly we reduce Weighted MIN SAT$(\mathcal{F})$ to MIN SAT$(\mathcal{F})$.

Given an instance $\mathcal{I}$ of Weighted MAX ONES$(\mathcal{F})$ on variables $x_1, \ldots, x_n$, constraints $C_1, \ldots, C_m$ and weights $w_1, \ldots, w_n$, we create an instance $\mathcal{I}'$ of MAX ONES$(\mathcal{F})$ on variables $\{\{y_i^j\}_{j=1}^{w_i}\}_{i=1}^n$. For every constraint C_j of $\mathcal{I}$ of the form $f(x_{i_1}, \ldots, x_{i_k})$, and for every $j \in \{1, \ldots, k\}$ and $n_j \in \{1, \ldots, w_{i_j}\}$ we impose the constraints $f(y_{i_1}^{n_1}, \ldots, y_{i_k}^{n_k})$. We now claim that the reduced instance is essentially equivalent to the instance we started with. To see this, notice that given any feasible solution $\vec{y}$ to the $\mathcal{I}'$, we may convert it to another feasible solution $\vec{y}'$ in which, for every i, all the variables $\{(\vec{y}')_i^j | j = 1, \ldots, w_i\}$ have the same assignment, by setting $(\vec{y}')_i^j$ to 1, if any of the variables $y_i^{j'}$, $j' = 1, \ldots, w_i$ is set to 1. Notice that this preserves feasibility and only increases the contribution to the objective function. The assignment $\vec{y}'$ now induces an assignment to $\vec{x}$ with the same value of the objective function. Thus the reduced instance is essentially equivalent to the original one. This concludes the reduction from Weighted MAX ONES$(\mathcal{F})$ to MAX ONES$(\mathcal{F})$. The reduction from Weighted MIN ONES$(\mathcal{F})$ to MIN ONES$(\mathcal{F})$ is similar. □

7.2   The class (Weighted) MAX SAT

We now establish that every (Weighted) MAX SAT$(\mathcal{F})$ problem is either in P or APX-complete. The following lemma establishes sufficient conditions for the polynomial time solvability of Weighted MAX SAT$(\mathcal{F})$.

Lemma 7.3 [PO containment] *If $\mathcal{F}$ is 0-valid or 1-valid or 2-monotone,* Weighted MAX SAT$(\mathcal{F})$ *is in* PO.

Proof: If every constraint in $\mathcal{F}$ is 0-valid (1-valid), then the assignment which assigns a zero (one) to every variable trivially satisfies all the constraints. Otherwise, if every constraint is 2-monotone, any given input instance can be transformed into a weighted instance of the *s-t* MIN CUT problem such that a minimum cut corresponds to an assignment minimizing the weight of unsatisfied constraints and correspondingly, an assignment minimizing the weight of unsatisfied constraints, represents a minimum weight *s-t* cut (see [17, 54] for details). □

We will use the following result to identify APX-hard Weighted MAX SAT$(\mathcal{F})$ problems.

Lemma 7.4 [74, 52] MAX SAT$(\{\text{XOR}\})$ *is* APX-*hard.*

Combining the above with Lemma 5.37 and Corollary 5.19, we obtain the following lemma.

Lemma 7.5 [APX-hardness] *If $\mathcal{F}$ is not 0-valid or 1-valid or 2-monotone, then* MAX SAT$(\mathcal{F})$ *is* APX-*hard.*

Proof: By Lemma 5.37, we have that $\mathcal{F}$ strictly implements the function XOR. Combined with Corollary 5.19 and Lemma 7.4 above, we get that MAX SAT$(\mathcal{F})$ is APX-hard.   □

Note that the APX containment of Weighted MAX SAT$(\mathcal{F})$ was already proved in Proposition 5.17. Combined with Lemmas 7.3 and 7.5, we get the following dichotomy theorem for (Weighted) MAX SAT$(\mathcal{F})$.

Theorem 7.6 [MAX SAT classification theorem] [17, 54] *For any constraint set $\mathcal{F}$, (Weighted) MAX SAT$(\mathcal{F})$ is either in* P *or is* APX-*complete. Moreover, it is in* P *if and only if $\mathcal{F}$ is either 0-valid or 1-valid or 2-monotone.*

7.3   The class (Weighted) MAX ONES

In contrast to the class MAX SAT, the class MAX ONES captures some problems for which it is NP-hard to find even a feasible solution (i.e., problems that are not decidable in polynomial time). At the same time, the class contains many problems that are either easy to solve exactly or are approximable to within constant factors. Consequently, our classification theorem for this class exhibits a richer structure, as described below.

Theorem 7.7 [MAX ONES classification theorem] [56] *For every constraint set $\mathcal{F}$, (Weighted) MAX ONES$(\mathcal{F})$ is either solvable exactly in* PO *or* APX-*complete or poly-APX-complete or decidable but not approximable to within any factor or not decidable. Furthermore,*

1. *if $\mathcal{F}$ is 1-valid or weakly positive or affine with width 2, then (Weighted) MAX ONES$(\mathcal{F})$ is in* PO.

2. *Else if $\mathcal{F}$ is affine, then (Weighted) MAX ONES$(\mathcal{F})$ is* APX-*complete.*

3. *Else if $\mathcal{F}$ is weakly negative or bijunctive, then (Weighted) MAX ONES$(\mathcal{F})$ is poly-APX complete.*

4. *Else if $\mathcal{F}$ is 0-valid, then the task of finding a feasible solution to (Weighted) MAX ONES$(\mathcal{F})$ is in* P *but finding a solution of positive value is* NP-*hard.*

5. *Else the task of finding any feasible solution to MAX ONES$(\mathcal{F})$ is* NP-*hard.*

7.3.1   Preliminaries

In this subsection, we prove a few preliminary lemmas that we will need in the proof of the theorem, particularly in cases 2 and 3. We first show that, in these cases, it is essentially equivalent for us to consider the weighted or unweighted MAX ONES$(\mathcal{F})$ problem.

We begin with a slightly stronger definition of polynomial-time solvability of SAT$(\mathcal{F})$ than we will need. We then show that given this stronger form of SAT$(\mathcal{F})$ that insofar as APX-hardness and poly-APX-hardness are concerned, the weighted and unweighted cases of MAX ONES$(\mathcal{F})$ are equivalent. We conclude by showing that in cases 2 and 3 the stronger form of SAT$(\mathcal{F})$ holds.

Definition 7.8 *We say that a constraint satisfaction problem SAT$(\mathcal{F})$ is strongly decidable if given m constraints on n variables $x_1, \ldots, x_n$ and an index $i \in \{1, \ldots, n\}$, there exists a polynomial time algorithm which decides if there exists an assignment to $x_1, \ldots, x_n$ satisfying all m constraints and additionally satisfying the property $x_i = 1$.*

Lemma 7.9 *If $\mathcal{F}$ is a strongly decidable constraint family the* Weighted MAX ONES($\mathcal{F}$) *AP-reduces to* MAX ONES($\mathcal{F}$).

Proof: By Lemma 7.2 it suffices to show that Weighted MAX ONES($\mathcal{F}$) is in poly-APX, and this is shown in Lemma 7.10.   □

Lemma 7.10 *If $\mathcal{F}$ is a strongly decidable constraint family, then* Weighted MAX ONES($\mathcal{F}$) *is in* poly-APX.

Proof: We give an n-approximation algorithm for this problem. Given an instance of MAX ONES($\mathcal{F}$) with variables $x_1, \ldots, x_n$, constraints $C_1, \ldots, C_m$ and (without loss of generality) weights $w_1 \leq w_2 \cdots \leq w_n$, we find the largest index i such that the instance is still satisfiable with $x_i = 1$. We output such a satisfying assignment. The objective we achieve is at least w_i, while the optimum is at most $\sum_{j=1}^{i} w_j \leq i w_i \leq n w_i$. Thus we have an n-approximation algorithm for Weighted MAX ONES($\mathcal{F}$).   □

The ability to work with weighted problems in combination with Lemma 5.20 allows us to use existential quantification over auxiliary variables and the notion of perfect implementations of constraints.

As our examination will eventually show, there is really no essential difference in the approximability of the weighted and unweighted problems. For now we will satisfy ourselves by stating this conditionally.

Corollary 7.11 *For any strongly decidable constraint set $\mathcal{F}$,* MAX ONES($\mathcal{F}$) *is APX-hard if and only if the* Weighted MAX ONES($\mathcal{F}$) *is APX-hard. Similarly,* MAX ONES($\mathcal{F}$) *is poly-APX-hard if and only if* Weighted MAX ONES($\mathcal{F}$) *is poly-APX-hard.*

Before concluding we show that most problems of interest to us will be able to use the equivalence between weighted and unweighted problems.

Lemma 7.12 *If $\mathcal{F}$ is 1-valid or affine or weakly positive or weakly negative or bijunctive, then $\mathcal{F}$ is strongly decidable.*

Proof: For a constraint $f \in \mathcal{F}$ and an index $i \in \{1, \ldots, k\}$, let f_i^* be the constraint

$$f_i^*(x_1, \ldots, x_k) \stackrel{\text{def}}{=} f(x_1, \ldots, x_{i-1}, 1, x_{i+1}, \ldots, x_k).$$

Further let $\mathcal{F}^*$ be the constraint set

$$\mathcal{F}^* \stackrel{\text{def}}{=} \mathcal{F} \cup \{f_i^* | f \in \mathcal{F}, i \in [k]\}.$$

First observe that the problem of strong decidability of $\mathcal{F}$ is the decision problem SAT($\mathcal{F}^*$). Further, observe that if $\mathcal{F}$ is 1-valid or weakly positive or weakly negative or affine or bijunctive, the so is $\mathcal{F}^*$.

Thus in each case we end up with a problem from SAT($\mathcal{F}$) which is in P by Schaefer's theorem, Theorem 6.2.   □

7.3.2   Containment results (algorithms) for MAX ONES

Note that the poly-APXcontainment for case 3 has already been dealt with in Lemma 7.10. For case 4, the fact that the all zero assignment is feasible shows that it is easy to find a feasible solution to the Weighted MAX ONES($\mathcal{F}$) problem. Thus it suffices to show membership in PO for Case 1 and membership in APX for case 2. We deal with these two cases in the next two lemmas.

Lemma 7.13 [PO containment] Weighted MAX ONES($\mathcal{F}$) *is in* PO *if* $\mathcal{F}$ *is 1-valid or is weakly positive or is affine with width 2.*

Proof: If $\mathcal{F}$ is 1-valid, then setting each variable to 1 satisfies all constraint applications with the maximum possible variable weight.

If $\mathcal{F}$ is weakly positive, then the problem of finding the feasible assignment with the greatest weight of one is similar to the problem of finding the minimal model of a Horn formula. This can be done in linear time by using unit resolution (see, for instance, [71]).

In the case that $\mathcal{F}$ is affine with width 2, we reduce the problem of finding a feasible solution to checking whether a graph is bipartite, and then use the bipartition to find the optimal solution. Notice that each constraint corresponds to a conjunction of constraints of the form $x_i = x_j$ or $x_i \neq x_j$. Create a vertex x_j for each variable x_j and for each constraint $x_i \neq x_j$, add an edge (x_i, x_j). For each constraint $x_i = x_j$, identify the vertices x_i and x_j; if this creates a self-loop, then clearly no feasible assignment is possible. Check whether the graph is bipartite; if not, then there is no feasible assignment. If so, then for each connected component of the graph choose the side with larger weight in the bipartition, and set the variables corresponding to this side to one. $\square$

Lemma 7.14 [APX containment] *If* $\mathcal{F}$ *is affine, then the* Weighted MAX ONES($\mathcal{F}$) *is in* APX.

Proof: By Lemmas 7.12 and 7.9 it suffices to consider the unweighted case. In this case when all constraints are affine, then satisfying all constraints is essentially the problem of solving a linear system of equations over $GF(2)$. If the system is overdetermined, then no feasible solution exists, else setting some of variables arbitrarily determines the remainder of the solution. To be more precise, the variables $\vec{x}$ can be partitioned into $\vec{x'}$ and $\vec{x''}$ such that the feasible solutions are given by arbitrary assignment to $\vec{x''}$ and setting $\vec{x'} = A\vec{x''} \oplus \vec{b}$ for some 0/1 matrix A and some 0/1 vector b (where matrix arithmetic is carried out over $GF(2)$). Setting the variables in $\vec{x''}$ to 1 with probability 1/2 we find that for any variable x_i whose assignment is not a constant in all feasible solutions, x_i is set to 1 w.p. 1/2. Thus the expected number of ones is at least OPT/2, giving a 2-approximate solution. $\square$

7.3.3   Hardness results for MAX ONES

We now move on to showing the hardness results for Theorem 7.7. Note that there is nothing to be shown in case 1 and that case 5 follows directly from Schaefer's theorem (Theorem 6.2). Note also that case 4 follows immediately from Proposition 6.11, which shows that finding a non-zero feasible assignment is NP-hard. In what follows, we deal with the two remaining cases (case 2 and case 3).

The APX-hard case

We start by showing that the problems in case 2 are APX-hard. The basic idea of this proof is to show via implementations that MAX CUT can be reduced to any such problem. We first show that two basic problems in this case are APX-hard by reducing MAX CUT to them.

Lemma 7.15 Weighted MAX ONES($\{XNOR_3\}$) *is* APX-*hard.*

Proof: We reduce the MAX CUT problem to the weighted MAX ONES($\{XOR_3\}$) problem as follows. Given a graph $G = (V, E)$ we create a variable x_v for every vertex $v \in V$ and a variable x_e for every edge $e \in E$. The weight w_v associated with the vertex variable x_v is 0. The weight w_e of an edge variable x_e is 1. For every edge e between u and v we create the constraint $x_e \oplus x_u \oplus x_v = 0$. It is clear that any 0/1 assignment to the x_v's define a cut and for an edge $e = \{u, v\}$, x_e is one if and only if u and v are on opposite sides of the cut. Thus solutions to the MAX ONES problem correspond to cuts in G with the objective function being the number of edges crossing the cut. □

Lemma 7.16 Weighted MAX ONES($\{XNOR_4, XOR\}$) *is* APX-*hard.*

Proof: We reduce MAX CUT to Weighted MAX ONES($\{XNOR_4, XOR\}$). Given a graph $G = (V, E)$, we create an instance $\mathcal{I}$ of Weighted MAX ONES($\{XNOR_4, XOR\}$) with variables x_v for every $v \in V$, x_e for every $e \in E$, one global variable z (which is supposed to be zero) and $m \triangleq |E|$ auxiliary variables $y_1, \ldots, y_m$. The constraints of $\mathcal{I}$ are as follows: For every edge $e = \{u, v\}$ in G we impose the constraint $XNOR_4(x_e, x_u, x_v, z)$. In addition we include the constraint $XOR(z, y_i)$ for every $i \in \{1, \ldots, m\}$. Finally we set the weights of the vertex variables and z to be zero and the weights of the edge variables and the auxiliary variables y_i to 1.

We first notice that the optimum of $\mathcal{I}$ is exactly MAX CUT(G) + m: Any assignment with $z = 1$ attains an objective of at most m, while any assignment with $z = 1$ defines a cut and attains an objective of $m+$ number of edges crossing the cut.

Let s be an r-approximate solution to $\mathcal{I}$. Notice that objective attained by s is at least (MAX CUT(G) + m)/r. If $r > 6/5$, we pick a greedy solution which gives a 2-approximate to MAX CUT(G), which is an $1 + 5(r - 1)$-approximate solution. Else, if $r \leq 6/5$, we report the cut with one side of the partition being vertices who are assigned to 0 and the other side consisting of vertices who are assigned to 1. We claim such a cut must have at least (MAX CUT(G) + m)/$r - m$ edges crossing the cut. Using $m \leq 2$MAX CUT(G) and $r \leq 6/5$, we find this number is at least MAX CUT(G)/r', where $r' \leq 1 + 5(r - 1)$. Thus in either case the reduction satisfies the properties required by an AP-reduction. The lemma follows. □

We are now ready to show APX-hardness for this case.

Lemma 7.17 [APX-hardness] *If $\mathcal{F}$ is affine but not of width-2 nor 1-valid, then $\mathcal{F}$ perfectly implements the family $\{XNOR_4, XOR\}$ or the function $XNOR_3$. Thus,* MAX ONES($\mathcal{F}$) *is* APX-*hard.*

Proof: By Lemma 5.34, $\mathcal{F}$ implements $XNOR_4$ perfectly. Let $f \in \mathcal{F}$ be a non 1-valid function. If f is C-closed, then by Lemma 5.24 f implements XOR and thus $\mathcal{F}$ implements the set $\{XNOR_4, XOR\}$. Using Lemmas 5.20 and 7.16, we conclude that Weighted MAX ONES($\mathcal{F}$)

is APX-hard and then use Lemma 7.12 and Corollary 7.11 to conclude that MAX ONES($\mathcal{F}$) is APX-hard.

Now consider the case when f is not C-closed. Here, we can apply Lemma 5.25 (part 2) to find that f implements F perfectly. In such a case we use $\text{XNOR}_4(x_1, x_2, x_3, z)$ and $\text{F}(z)$ to implement the constraint $\text{XNOR}_3(x_1, x_2, x_3)$. Thus, we are now done, using Lemma 7.15. $\square$

The poly-APX-hard case

The hard problem we will use for this part is MAX CLIQUE which was shown to be hard to approximate to within polynomial factors by the sequence of works [29, 4, 3]. This implies that MAX CLIQUE is poly-APX-hard, as shown by [52].

Proposition 7.18 MAX ONES($\{\text{OR}_2\}$) *is poly-APX-hard.*

Proof: It turns out this problem is exactly the MAX CLIQUE problem. Given a graph G, let $\mathcal{I}$ be the instance of MAX ONES($\{\text{OR}_2\}$) with variables $\{x_v | v$ is a vertex of $G\}$ and constraints $\bar{x}_u \wedge \bar{x}_v$ if and only if (u, v) is *not* an edge of G. The set of variables that are assigned 1 in any satisfying assignment then correspond to a clique, and the objective is the size of the clique. The proposition follows from the fact that MAX CLIQUE is poly-APX-hard [29, 4, 3, 52]. $\square$

The proof for the poly-APX-hardness is somewhat long. We start by proving a lemma that implies Weighted MAX ONES($\mathcal{F} \cup \{\text{F}, \text{T}\}$) is poly-APX-hard.

Lemma 7.19 *If $\mathcal{F}$ is not weakly positive or affine, then $\mathcal{F} \cup \{\text{F}, \text{T}\}$ perfectly implements* OR_2.

Proof: Since $\mathcal{F}$ is not weakly positive, we have by Lemma 5.26 that $\mathcal{F} \cup \{\text{F}, \text{T}\}$ perfectly implement OR_2 or XOR. In the former case we are done. In the latter case we use the fact that $\mathcal{F}$ is not affine along with Lemma 5.30 to conclude that $\mathcal{F} \cup \{\text{F}, \text{T}\}$ perfectly implements one of OR_0, OR_1 or OR_2. Combined with XOR, we find that any of these functions implement OR_2. For example, $\text{OR}_0(\bar{x}, \bar{y})$, $\text{XOR}(x, \bar{x})$ and $\text{XOR}(y, \bar{y})$ give a perfect 3-implementation of $\text{OR}_2(x, y)$. $\square$

Now all that remains to be done is to implement F and T. Lemma 5.24 shows that $\mathcal{F}$ does implement F. Unfortunately implementing T may not always be possible. For example, all functions in $\mathcal{F}$ may be 0-valid! We will find two alternates for such an event: (1) If $\mathcal{F}$ implements OR_2, then we don't need to implement T. (2) If $\mathcal{F}$ implements OR_1, then we will show that this is good enough to simulate T. We won't get an implementation of T, however we will get an AP-reduction from Weighted MAX ONES($\mathcal{F} \cup \{\text{T}\}$) to Weighted MAX ONES($\mathcal{F} \cup \{\text{OR}_1\}$). The following lemmas formalize the above.

Lemma 7.20 *If f is bijunctive and C-closed, then f is affine with width 2.*

Proof: We run through the maxterms of f and show that each one can be replaced by an affine constraint of width two. Since maxterms of size 1 are already affine with width two, we may move on the maxterms of size 1. Say, $x_1 \vee \bar{x}_2$ is a maxterm of f. Then C-closedness of f implies that the complementary term $\bar{x}_1 \vee x_2$ is also a maxterm of f. Thus we can replace $x_1 \vee \bar{x}_2$ by the stronger constraint $x_1 \oplus x_2 = 0$ which is affine with width two. $\square$

Lemma 7.21 *If $\mathcal{F}$ is 0-valid or weakly negative or bijunctive, but $\mathcal{F}$ is not 1-valid, nor affine nor weakly positive, then $\mathcal{F}$ implements* F.

Proof: By Lemma 5.24 it suffices to show that $\mathcal{F}$ is not 1-valid and not C-closed. The former is given and we now prove the latter.

Notice that a C-closed 0-valid constraint is also 1-valid. A C-closed weakly positive constraint will also be weakly negative. Lastly, a C-closed bijunctive constraint is an affine constraint of width 2 (by Lemma 7.20). Thus, if $\mathcal{F}$ is 0-valid, then the constraint which is not 1-valid is not C-closed. If $\mathcal{F}$ is weakly negative, the constraint which is not weakly positive is not C-closed. Similarly if $\mathcal{F}$ is bijunctive, then the constraint that is not affine is not C-closed.   □

Lemma 7.22 *If $\mathcal{F}$ is 0-valid or weakly negative or bijunctive, but $\mathcal{F}$ is not 1-valid, nor affine nor weakly positive, then $\mathcal{F}$ implements at least one of* T, OR_1, OR_2.

Proof: We already have by Lemma 7.21 that $\mathcal{F}$ implements F. Let g be a non-affine function from $\mathcal{F}$. If g is 0-valid, then we are done by Lemma 5.30 which says that $\{g, \mathsf{F}\}$ (and hence $\mathcal{F}$) implements OR_1 or OR_2. Else g is not 0-valid in which case $\mathcal{F}$ implements T.   □

Finally we deal with the case where we have an implementation of OR_1.

Lemma 7.23 *For any family $\mathcal{F}$* Weighted MAX ONES$(\mathcal{F} \cup \{\mathsf{T}\})$ *AP-reduces to* Weighted MAX ONES$(\mathcal{F} \cup \{\mathsf{OR}_1\})$.

Proof: Given an instance $\mathcal{I}$ of Weighted MAX ONES$(\mathcal{F} \cup \{\mathsf{T}\})$ we construct an instance $\mathcal{I}'$ of Weighted MAX ONES$(\mathcal{F} \cup \{x \vee \bar{y}\})$ as follows. The variable set of $\mathcal{I}'$ is the same as that of $\mathcal{I}$. Every constraint from $\mathcal{F}$ in $\mathcal{I}$ is also included in $\mathcal{I}'$. The only remaining constraints are of the form $\mathsf{T}(x_i)$ for some variables x_i. We simulate this constraint in $\mathcal{I}'$ with $n-1$ constraints of the form $x_i \vee \bar{x}_j$ for every $j \in \{1, \ldots, n\}$, $j \neq i$. Every non-zero solution to the resulting instance $\mathcal{I}'$ is also a solution to $\mathcal{I}$, since the solution must have $x_i = 1$ or else every $x_j = 0$. Thus the resulting instance of Weighted MAX ONES$(\mathcal{F} \cup \{x \vee \bar{y}\})$ has the same objective function and the same feasible space and is hence at least as hard as the original problem.   □

We are finally ready to prove the poly-APX-hardness lemma.

Lemma 7.24 (poly-APX-hardness) *If $\mathcal{F}$ is weakly negative or bijunctive, but $\mathcal{F}$ is not 1-valid, nor affine nor weakly positive, then* MAX ONES$(\mathcal{F})$ *is poly-APX-hard.*

Proof: Note that, by Lemma 7.12, $\mathcal{F}$ is strongly decidable and hence, by Lemma 7.9, Weighted MAX ONES$(\mathcal{F})$ AP-reduces to MAX ONES$(\mathcal{F})$. Thus it suffices to prove poly-APX-hardness for Weighted MAX ONES$(\mathcal{F})$.

By Lemma 7.22, we have that $\mathcal{F}$ implements one of the three functions OR_2, OR_1 or T. In the first case, we are done, so we move on to the remaining two. We also have by Lemma 7.21 that $\mathcal{F}$ implements F and so if we are in the case where $\mathcal{F}$ implements T, then we have that $\mathcal{F}$ implements $\mathcal{F} \cup \{\mathsf{F}, \mathsf{T}\}$; which, by Lemma 7.19, implements OR_2. So we are left with the case where $\mathcal{F}$ implements OR_1. In this case we have

Weighted MAX ONES$(\{\mathsf{OR}_2\}) \leq_{\mathrm{AP}}$ Weighted MAX ONES$(\mathcal{F} \cup \{\mathsf{F}, \mathsf{T}\})$

$\leq_{\mathrm{AP}}$ Weighted MAX ONES$(\mathcal{F} \cup \{\mathsf{OR}_1, \mathsf{F}\})$ (Using Lemma 7.23)

$\leq_{\mathrm{AP}}$ Weighted MAX ONES$(\mathcal{F})$

$\leq_{\mathrm{AP}}$ MAX ONES$(\mathcal{F})$.

Thus in all cases we are done.   □

7.4   The class (Weighted) MIN SAT

In this section we classify the class MIN SAT. In contrast to the results in previous sections, in this section (and the next) we will not be able to precisely determine the approximability of every problem in the class. However, we will still be able to partition the class into finitely many subclasses; and within each subclass, the problems are equivalent up to A-reducibility.

To define these subclasses, we use the notation "Π-completeness". Given optimization problems Π and Π′, we say Π′ is Π-complete if Π A-reduces to Π′ and vice versa. The MIN SAT classification theorem highlights four problems as important ones:

- MIN UNCUT = MIN SAT({XOR}). This problem has been studied previously by Klein et al. [57] and Garg, Vazirani, and Yannakakis [34]. The problem is known to be APX-hard and hence not approximable to within some constant factor greater than 1. On the other hand, the problem is known to be approximable to within a factor of $O(\log n)$ [34].

- MIN 2CNF DELETION = MIN SAT({OR_0, OR_2}). This problem has been studied by Klein et al. [58]. They show that the problem is APX-hard and that it is approximable to within a factor of $O(\log n \log \log n)$.

- NEAREST CODEWORD = MIN SAT({XOR, REP}). This is a classical problem for which hardness of approximation results have been shown by Arora et al. [1]. The MIN ONES version of this problem is essentially identical to this problem. For both problems, the hardness result of Arora et al. [1] shows that approximating this problem to within a factor of $\Omega(2^{\log^{1-\epsilon} n})$ is hard for every $\epsilon > 0$, unless NP $\subset$ DTIME($2^{\log^{O(1)} n}$). No nontrivial approximation guarantees are known for this problem (the trivial bound being a factor of m, which is easily achieved, since deciding if all equations are satisfiable amounts to solving a linear system).

- Lastly we also mention one more problem which is required to present our main theorem. MIN HORN DELETION = MIN SAT({$OR_{3,1}, F, T$}).

  This problem is essentially as hard as the NEAREST CODEWORD.

We now state the MIN SAT Classification Theorem.

Theorem 7.25 [MIN SAT classification theorem] [55] *For any constraint family $\mathcal{F}$, the problem* (Weighted) MIN SAT($\mathcal{F}$) *is in* PO *or is* APX-complete *or* MIN UNCUT-complete *or* MIN 2CNF DELETION-complete *or* NEAREST CODEWORD-complete *or* MIN HORN DELETION-complete *or the decision problem is* NP-hard. *Furthermore,*

1. *if $\mathcal{F}$ is 0-valid or 1-valid or 2-monotone, then* (Weighted) MIN SAT($\mathcal{F}$) *is in* PO.

2. *Else if $\mathcal{F}$ is IHS-B, then* (Weighted) MIN SAT($\mathcal{F}$) *is* APX-complete.

3. *Else if $\mathcal{F}$ is width-2 affine, then* (Weighted) MIN SAT($\mathcal{F}$) *is* MIN UNCUT-complete.

4. *Else if $\mathcal{F}$ is bijunctive, then* (Weighted) MIN SAT($\mathcal{F}$) *is* MIN 2CNF DELETION-complete.

5. *Else if $\mathcal{F}$ is affine, then* (Weighted) MIN SAT($\mathcal{F}$) *is* NEAREST CODEWORD-complete.

6. *Else if $\mathcal{F}$ is weakly positive or weakly negative, then* (Weighted) MIN SAT($\mathcal{F}$) *is* MIN HORN DELETION-complete.

7. *Else deciding if the optimum value of an instance of* (Weighted) MIN SAT($\mathcal{F}$) *is zero is* NP-complete.

7.4.1 Preliminary results

We start with an obvious equivalence between the complexity of the (Weighted) MIN SAT problem for a function family and its "complement". For a constraint f, let f^- denote the function $f^-(x) = f(\bar{x})$. For a family $\mathcal{F}$, let $\mathcal{F}^- = \{f^- | f \in \mathcal{F}\}$.

Proposition 7.26 *For every constraint family $\mathcal{F}$,* (Weighted) MIN SAT$(\mathcal{F})$ *is AP-reducible to* (Weighted) MIN SAT$(\mathcal{F}^-)$.

Proof: The reduction substitutes every constraint $f(\vec{x})$ from $\mathcal{F}$ with the constraint $f^-(\vec{x})$ from $\mathcal{F}^-$. A solution for the latter problem is converted into a solution for the former one by complementing the value of each variable. The transformation preserves the cost of the solution.   □

Proposition 7.27 *If $\mathcal{F}$ is decidable, then* Weighted MIN SAT$(\mathcal{F})$ *is in* poly-APX *and is AP-reducible to* MIN SAT$(\mathcal{F})$.

Proof: Given an instance $\mathcal{I}$ of Weighted MIN ONES$(\mathcal{F})$ with constraints $C_1, \ldots, C_m$ sorted in order of decreasing weight $w_1 \geq \cdots \geq w_m$. Let j be the largest index such that the constraints $C_1, \ldots, C_j$ are simultaneously satisfiable. Notice that j is computable in polynomial time and an assignment $\vec{a}$ satisfying $C_1, \ldots, C_j$ is computable in polynomial time. Then the solution $\vec{a}$ is an m-approximate solution to $\mathcal{I}$, since every solution must fail to satisfy at least one of the constraints $C_1, \ldots, C_{j+1}$ and thus have an objective of at least w_{j+1}, while $\vec{a}$ achieves an objective of at most $\sum_{i=j+1}^{m} w_i \leq m w_{j+1}$. Thus we conclude that Weighted MIN SAT$(\mathcal{F})$ is in poly-APX. The second part of the proposition follows by Lemma 7.2.   □

7.4.2 Containment results (algorithms) for MIN SAT

We now show the containment results described in Theorem 7.25. Most results described here are simple containment results which follow easily from the notion of a "basis". The more interesting result here is a constant factor approximation algorithm for IHS-B which is presented in Lemma 7.29.

We start with the classes contained in PO.

Lemma 7.28 [PO containment] *If $\mathcal{F}$ is 0-valid or 1-valid or 2-monotone, then* Weighted MIN SAT$(\mathcal{F}) \in$ PO.

Proof: The lemma may be proven directly as in the proof of Lemma 7.3. Alternately, one may use the equivalence of computing the exact optimum solution of Weighted MAX SAT$(\mathcal{F})$ and Weighted MIN SAT$(\mathcal{F})$, since for any given instance $\mathcal{I}$ of Weighted MAX SAT$(\mathcal{F})$ and the same instance to Weighted MIN SAT$(\mathcal{F})$ an optimum solution to one is also the optimum solution to the other. With this observation, the lemma follows from Lemma 7.3.   □

We now move on to APX containment results.

Lemma 7.29 [APX containment] *If $\mathcal{F}$ is IHS-B, then* Weighted MIN SAT$(\mathcal{F}) \in$ APX.

Proof: By Propositions 5.40 and 7.26 it suffices to prove the lemma for the problem Weighted MIN SAT(IHS-B), where IHS-$B = \{\mathsf{OR}_{k,0} | k \in [B]\} \cup \{\mathsf{OR}_1, \mathsf{F}\}$. We will show that for every B, Weighted MIN SAT(IHS-B) is $B + 1$-approximable.

Given an instance $\mathcal{I}$ of Weighted MIN SAT(IHS-B) on variables $x_1, \ldots, x_n$ with constraints $C_1, \ldots, C_m$ with weights $w_1, \ldots, w_m$, we create a linear program on variables $y_1, \ldots, y_n$ (corresponding to the Boolean variables $x_1, \ldots, x_n$) and variables $z_1, \ldots, z_m$ (corresponding to the constraints $C_1, \ldots, C_m$). For every constraint C_j in the instance $\mathcal{I}$ we create a LP constraint using the following transformation rules:

$$
\begin{array}{rcl}
C_j \ : \ x_{i_1} \vee \cdots \vee x_{i_k}, \text{ for } k \leq B & \to & z_j + y_{i_1} + \cdots + y_{i_k} \geq 1 \\
C_j \ : \ \bar{x}_{i_1} \vee x_{i_2} & \to & z_j + (1 - y_{i_1}) + y_{i_2} \geq 1 \\
C_j \ : \ \bar{x}_{i_1} & \to & z_j + (1 - y_{i_1}) \geq 1.
\end{array}
$$

In addition, we add the constraints $0 \leq z_j, y_i \leq 1$ for every i, j. It may be verified that any integer solution to the above LP corresponds to an assignment to the MIN SAT problem with the variable z_j set to 1 if the constraint C_j is not satisfied. Thus the objective function for the LP is to minimize $\sum_j w_j z_j$.

Given any feasible solution vector $y_1, \ldots, y_n, z_1, \ldots, z_m$ to the LP above, we show how to obtain a 0/1 vector $y_1'', \ldots, y_n'', z_1'', \ldots, z_m''$ that is also feasible such that $\sum_j w_j z_j'' \leq (B+1) \sum_j w_j z_j$.

First we set $y_i' = \min\{1, (B+1)y_i\}$ and $z_j' = \min\{1, (B+1)z_j\}$. Observe that the vector $y_1', \ldots, y_n', z_1', \ldots, z_m'$ is also feasible and gives a solution of value at most $(B+1) \sum_j w_j z_j$. We now show how to get an *integral* solution whose value is at most $\sum_j w_j z_j'$. For this part we first set $y_i'' = 1$ if $y_i' = 1$ and $z_j'' = 1$ if $z_i' = 1$. Now we remove every constraint in the LP that is made redundant. Notice in particular that every constraint of type (1) is now redundant (either z_j'' or one of the y_i'''s has already been set to 1 and hence the constraint will be satisfied by any assignment to the remaining variables). We now observe that, on the remaining variables, the LP constructed above reduces to the following

$$
\begin{array}{rrcl}
\text{Minimize} & \sum_j w_j z_j & & \\
\text{Subject to} & y_{i_2} - y_{i_1} + z_j & \geq & 0 \\
& y_{i_2} + z_j & \geq & 1 \\
& -y_{i_1} + z_j & \geq & 0
\end{array}
$$

with the y_i''s and z_j''s forming a feasible solution to the above LP. Notice further that every z_j occurs in at most one constraint above. Thus the above LP represents a s-t min cut problem, and therefore has an optimal integral solution. We set z_j'''s and y_i'' to such an integral and optimal solution. Notice that the so obtained solution is integral and satisfies $\sum_j w_j z_j'' \leq \sum_j w_j z_j' \leq (B+1) \sum_j w_j z_j$.   □

Lemma 7.30 [MIN UNCUT containment] *For any family $\mathcal{F}$ that is affine with width* 2, Weighted MIN SAT($\mathcal{F}$) *A-reduces to* MIN SAT($\{$XOR$\}$).

Proof: First we will argue that the family $\mathcal{F}' = \{$XOR, F, T$\}$ perfectly implements $\mathcal{F}$. By Proposition 5.40 it suffices to implement the basic width-2 affine functions: namely, the functions XOR, REP, F and T. Every function except XOR is already present in $\mathcal{F}'$. Further, the constraints XOR(x, z) and XOR(z, y) perfectly implement the constraint REP(x, y).

We would be done if we could now show that $\{$XOR$\}$ perfectly implements the functions F and T, but this is not the case. So instead we resort to reductions directly and show, in Lemma 7.31, that Weighted MIN SAT($\mathcal{F}'$) A-reduces to Weighted MIN SAT($\{$XOR$\}$). (The lemma is more general and applies whenever the target is not 0-valid or 1-valid, which is certainly true for us.) Finally the weights can be removed using Proposition 7.27.   □

Lemma 7.31 *If $\mathcal{F}$ is not 0-valid or 1-valid, then* Weighted MIN SAT$(\mathcal{F} \cup \{F, T\})$ *is A-reducible to* Weighted MIN SAT$(\mathcal{F})$.

Proof: Let f_0 be the function from $\mathcal{F}$ that is not 0-valid and let f_1 be the function that is not 1-valid. If some function g in $\mathcal{F}$ is not C-closed, then, by Lemma 5.24, $\mathcal{F}$ perfectly and strictly implements F and T. Hence, by Lemma 5.22, MIN SAT$(\mathcal{F} \cup \{F, T\})$ is A-reducible to MIN SAT$(\mathcal{F})$.

Otherwise, every function of $\mathcal{F}$ is C-closed and hence by Lemma 5.24, $\mathcal{F}$ perfectly and strictly implements the XOR function and hence the REP function. Thus it suffices to show that Weighted MIN SAT$(\mathcal{F} \cup \{F, T\})$ is A-reducible to Weighted MIN SAT$(\mathcal{F} \cup \{XOR, REP\})$ for C-closed families $\mathcal{F}$. Here we use an idea from [7] described next.

Given an instance $\mathcal{I}$ of Weighted MIN SAT$(\mathcal{F} \cup \{F, T\})$ on variables $x_1, \ldots, x_n$ and constraints $C_1, \ldots, C_m$, we define an instance $\mathcal{I}'$ of Weighted MIN SAT$(\mathcal{F})$ whose variables are $x_1, \ldots, x_n$ and, additionally, one new auxiliary variable x_F. Each constraint of the form $F(x_i)$ (resp., $T(x_i)$) in $\mathcal{I}$ is replaced by a constraint $REP(x_i, x_F)$ (resp., $XOR(x_i, x_F)$). All the other constraints are not changed. Thus $\mathcal{I}'$ also has m constraints. Given a solution $a_1, \ldots, a_n, a_F$ for $\mathcal{I}'$ that satisfies m' of these constraints, notice that the assignment $\bar{a}_1, \ldots, \bar{a}_n, \bar{a}_F$ also satisfies the same collection of constraints (since every function in $\mathcal{F}$ is C-closed). In one of these cases the assignment to x_F is false and then we notice that a constraint of $\mathcal{I}$ is satisfied if and only if the corresponding constraint in $\mathcal{I}'$ is satisfied. Thus every solution to $\mathcal{I}'$ can be mapped to a solution of $\mathcal{I}$ with the same contribution to the objective function. $\quad\square$

The following lemmas show reducibility to MIN 2CNF DELETION, NEAREST CODEWORD and MIN HORN DELETION.

Lemma 7.32 [MIN 2CNF DELETION containment] *For any family $\mathcal{F}$ that is bijunctive, the family $\{OR_0, OR_2\}$ perfectly implements every function in $\mathcal{F}$ and hence* Weighted MIN SAT$(\mathcal{F}) \leq_A$ MIN 2CNF DELETION.

Proof: Again it suffices to consider the basic constraints of $\mathcal{F}$ and this is some subset of

$$\{OR_0, OR_1, OR_2, F, T\}.$$

The family 2CNF contains the first and the third function. Since it contains a non 0-valid function, a non 1-valid function and a non C-closed function, it also perfectly implements F and T (by Lemma 5.24, Part 2). This leaves the function OR_1. It is easily seen that $OR_1(x, y)$ is perfectly implemented by the constraints $OR_2(x, z)$ and $OR_0(y, z)$. The A-reduction now follows from Lemma 5.22. $\quad\square$

Lemma 7.33 [NEAREST CODEWORD containment] *For any family $\mathcal{F}$ that is affine, the family $\{XOR_3, XNOR_3\}$ perfectly implements every function in $\mathcal{F}$, and thus* Weighted MIN SAT$(\mathcal{F}) \leq_A$ NEAREST CODEWORD.

Proof: It suffices to show perfect implementation of the basic affine constraints, namely, constraints of the form $XNOR_p$ and XOR_q for every $p, q \geq 1$. We focus on the former type, as the implementation of the latter is analogous. First, we observe that the constraint $REP(x_1, x_2) = XNOR_2(x_1, x_2)$ is perfectly implemented by the constraints $\{XNOR_3(x_1, x_2, z_1),$ $XNOR_3(x_1, x_2, z_2), XNOR_3(x_1, x_2, z_3), XNOR_3(z_1, z_2, z_3)\}$ Next, the constraint $F(x_1)$ can be perfectly implemented by $\{REP(x_1, z_1), REP(x_1, z_2), REP(x_1, z_3), XNOR_3(z_1, z_2, z_3)\}$ Finally, the constraint $XNOR_p(x_1, \ldots, x_p)$ for any $p > 3$ can be perfectly implemented as follows.

We introduce the following set of constraints using the auxiliary variables $z_1, z_2, \ldots, z_{p-2}$ and the set of constraints:

$$\{\mathsf{XNOR}_3(x_1, x_2, z_1), \mathsf{XNOR}_3(z_1, x_3, z_2), \mathsf{XNOR}_3(z_2, x_4, z_3), \ldots, \mathsf{XNOR}_3(z_{p-2}, x_{p-1}, x_p)\}. \quad \square$$

Lemma 7.34 [MIN HORN DELETION containment] *For any family $\mathcal{F}$ that is weakly positive the family $\{\mathsf{OR}_{3,1}, \mathsf{F}, \mathsf{T}\})$ perfectly implements every function in $\mathcal{F}$ and thus* Weighted MIN SAT$(\mathcal{F}) \leq_A$ MIN HORN DELETION.

Proof: As usual it suffices to perfectly implement every function in the basis $\{\mathsf{OR}_{k,0}\} \cup \{\mathsf{OR}_{k,1}\}$. The constraint $\mathsf{OR}_0(x, y)$ is perfectly implemented by the constraints $\mathsf{OR}_{3,1}(a, x, y)$ and $\mathsf{T}(a)$. $\mathsf{OR}_{2,1}(x, y)$ is perfectly implemented by $\mathsf{OR}_{3,1}(x, y, a)$ and $\mathsf{F}(a)$. The perfect implementation of $\mathsf{OR}_{3,0}(x, y, z)$ is $\mathsf{OR}_0(x, a)$ and $\mathsf{OR}_{3,1}(a, y, z)$ (the constraint $(a \vee x)$, in turn, may be implemented with the method already shown). Thus every k-ary constraint, for $k \leq 3$ can be perfectly implemented by the family $\{\mathsf{OR}_{3,1}, \mathsf{F}, \mathsf{T}\}$. For $k \geq 4$, we use the textbook reduction from SAT to 3SAT (see, e.g., [32, Page 49]) and we observe that when applied to k-ary weakly positive constraints it yields a perfect implementation using only 3-ary weakly positive constraints. $\quad \square$

To conclude this section we describe the trivial approximation algorithms for NEAREST CODEWORD and MIN HORN DELETION. They follow easily from Proposition 7.27 and the fact that both families are decidable.

Corollary 7.35 [to Proposition 7.27] MIN HORN DELETION *and* NEAREST CODEWORD *are in* poly-APX.

7.4.3   Hardness results (reductions) for MIN SAT

Lemma 7.36 [APX-hardness] *If $\mathcal{F}$ is not 0-valid or 1-valid or 2-monotone and $\mathcal{F}$ is IHS-B, then* MIN SAT$(\mathcal{F})$ *is APX-hard.*

Proof: The proof essentially follows from (the "only if" part of) Theorem 7.6 in combination with Proposition 5.17. We show that for every $\mathcal{F}$, MAX SAT$(\mathcal{F})$ AP-reduces to MIN SAT$(\mathcal{F})$. Let $\mathcal{I}$ be an instance of MAX SAT$(\mathcal{F})$ on n variables and m constraints. Let $\vec{x}'$ be a solution satisfying m/k constraints that can be found in polynomial time (by Proposition 5.17). Let $\vec{x}''$ be an r-approximate solution to the same instance $\mathcal{I}$ viewed as an instance of MIN SAT$(\mathcal{F})$. If OPT is the optimum solution to the maximization problem $\mathcal{I}$, then $\vec{x}''$ satisfies at least $m - r(m - \text{OPT}) = r\text{OPT} - (r - 1)m$ constraints. Thus the better of the two solutions is an r'-approximate solution to the instance $\mathcal{I}$ of MAX SAT$(\mathcal{F})$, where

$$
\begin{aligned}
r' &\leq \frac{\text{OPT}}{\max\{m/k, r\text{OPT} - (r-1)m\}} \\
&\leq \frac{((r-1)k + 1)\text{OPT}}{(r-1)k(m/k) + r\text{OPT} - (r-1)m} \\
&= \frac{1 + (r-1)k}{r} \\
&\leq 1 + (r-1)k.
\end{aligned}
$$

Thus MAX SAT$(\mathcal{F})$ AP-reduces to MIN SAT$(\mathcal{F})$. The lemma follows from the APX-hardness of MAX SAT$(\mathcal{F})$ (Theorem 7.6). $\quad \square$

Lemma 7.37 [MIN UNCUT-hardness] *If $\mathcal{F}$ is affine with width 2, but not 0-valid or 1-valid or 2-monotone or IHS-B, then* MIN SAT$(\mathcal{F})$ *is* MIN UNCUT*-hard.*

Proof: Recall that MIN UNCUT-hardness requires that MIN SAT(XOR) be A-reducible to MIN SAT$(\mathcal{F})$. In turn, it suffices to show that $\mathcal{F}$ perfectly implements XOR.

If $\mathcal{F}$ is C-closed, then by part 1 of Lemma 5.24, we have that $\mathcal{F}$ implements XOR. So we may assume $\mathcal{F}$ is not C-closed. In such a case, by part 2 of Lemma 5.24, we have that $\mathcal{F}$ implements both F and T. By Lemma 5.28, we now have that $\mathcal{F}$ perfectly implements XOR. □

Lemma 7.38 [MIN 2CNF DELETION-hardness] *If $\mathcal{F}$ is a bijunctive family that is not 0-valid or 1-valid or IHS-B or affine with width 2, then* MIN SAT$(\mathcal{F})$ *is* MIN 2CNF DELETION*-hard.*

Proof: Recall that we wish to show that MIN SAT($\{OR_0, OR_2\}$ A-reduces to MIN SAT$(\mathcal{F})$; or, in other words, $\mathcal{F}$ perfectly implements OR_0 and OR_2.

By Lemma 7.20, we have that every bijunctive family that is C-closed is affine with width 2. Since $\mathcal{F}$ is not affine, we have that it is not C-closed. Since $\mathcal{F}$ is not 0-valid or 1-valid, it perfectly implements both F and T (by part 2 of Lemma 5.24). Applying Lemmas 5.29 we have that $\mathcal{F}$ perfectly implements $\{OR_0, OR_2\}$ or it perfectly implements XOR. In the first case, we are done, else we use the fact that $\mathcal{F}$ is not affine with width 2. By Lemma 4.11, this implies that $\mathcal{F}$ is not affine (since every bijunctive function that is affine has width 2). Thus, using Lemma 5.30, we have that $\mathcal{F}$ perfectly implements one of the three functions OR_0, OR_1, OR_2. Combined with XOR, any of these functions perfectly implements both the functions OR_0 and OR_2. □

Lemma 7.39 (NEAREST CODEWORD-hardness) *If $\mathcal{F}$ is affine but not 0-valid or 1-valid or affine with width 2, then* MIN SAT$(\mathcal{F})$ *is* NEAREST CODEWORD*-hard.*

Proof: By Lemma 5.34 we know that in this case $\mathcal{F}$ perfectly implements the constraint $x_1 \oplus \cdots \oplus x_p = b$ for some $p \geq 3$ and some $b \in \{0, 1\}$. Thus the family $\mathcal{F} \cup \{F, T\}$ perfectly implements the functions $x \oplus y \oplus z = 0, x \oplus y \oplus z = 1$. Thus NEAREST CODEWORD = MIN SAT($\{x \oplus y \oplus z = 0, x \oplus y \oplus z = 1\}$) is A-reducible to MIN SAT$(\mathcal{F} \cup \{F, T\})$. Since $\mathcal{F}$ is neither 0-valid nor 1-valid, we can use Lemma 7.31 to conclude that MIN SAT$(\mathcal{F})$ is NEAREST CODEWORD-hard. □

The next lemma describes the best known hardness of approximation for the NEAREST CODEWORD problem. The result relies on an assumption stronger than NP $\neq$ P.

Lemma 7.40 [1] *For every $\epsilon > 0$,* NEAREST CODEWORD *is hard to approximate to within a factor of $\Omega(2^{\log^{1-\epsilon} n})$, unless NP has deterministic algorithms running in time $n^{\log^{O(1)} n}$.*

Proof: The required hardness of the nearest codeword problem is shown by Arora et al. [1]. The nearest codeword problem, as defined in Arora et al., works with the following problem: Given a $m \times n$ matrix A and a m-dimensional vector b, find an n-dimensional vector x which minimizes the Hamming distance between Ax and b. Thus this problem can be expressed as a MIN SAT problem with m affine constraints over n-variables. The only technical point to be noted is that these constraints have unbounded arity. In order to get rid of such long constraints, we replace a constraint of the form $x_1 \oplus \cdots \oplus x_l = 0$ into $l - 2$ constraints $x_1 \oplus x_2 \oplus z_1 = 0, z_1 \oplus x_3 \oplus z_2 = 0$, etc. on auxiliary variables $z_1, \ldots, z_{l-3}$. (The same implementation was used in Lemma 7.33.) This increases the number of constraints by a factor of at most n, but does not change the objective function. Thus, if M represents the number of constraints in the new instance of the problem, then the approximation hardness which is $2^{\log^{1-\epsilon} m}$ can be expressed as $2^{\frac{1}{2} \log^{1-\epsilon} M}$ which is still growing faster than, say, $2^{\log^{1-2\epsilon} M}$. Since the result of [1] holds for every positive ϵ, we still get the desired result claimed above.   □

It remains to see the MIN HORN DELETION-hard case.

Lemma 7.41 *If $\mathcal{F}$ is a C-closed family that is weakly positive or weakly negative, then $\mathcal{F}$ is a IHS-B family.*

Proof: Let f be a weakly positive (weakly negative) C-closed function. We claim that all of f's maxterms must be of the form $\mathsf{T}(x_i)$, $\mathsf{F}(x_i)$ or $\mathsf{OR}_1(x_i, x_j)$. If not, then since f is C-closed, the maxterm involving the complementary literals is also a maxterm of f, but the complementary maxterm is not weakly positive (and by Lemma 4.7 every maxterm of f must be weakly positive). But if all of f's maxterms are of the form $\mathsf{T}(x_i)$, $\mathsf{F}(x_i)$ or $\mathsf{OR}_{2,1}(x_i, x_j)$, then f is in IHS-B.   □

Lemma 7.42 [MIN HORN DELETION-hardness] *If $\mathcal{F}$ is weakly positive or weakly negative but not 0-valid or 1-valid or affine or bijunctive or IHS-B− or IHS-B+, then $\mathsf{MIN\ SAT}(\mathcal{F})$ is MIN HORN DELETION-hard.*

Proof: By Lemma 7.41, we have that $\mathcal{F}$ is not C-closed. Thus $\mathcal{F}$ perfectly implements both T and F. From Lemma 5.27 we now have that $\mathcal{F}$ perfectly implements $\mathsf{OR}_{3,1}$ or $\mathsf{OR}_{3,2}$. In the former case we have implemented every function in MIN HORN DELETION $= \{\mathsf{OR}_{3,1}, \mathsf{F}, \mathsf{T}\}$ and so we are done (using Lemma 5.22). In the latter case, we obtain an A-reduction from Weighted $\mathsf{MIN\ SAT}(\{\mathsf{OR}_{3,2}, \mathsf{F}, \mathsf{T}\}$ to Weighted $\mathsf{MIN\ SAT}(\mathcal{F})$. This is good enough, since we can now use Proposition 7.26 which shows that Weighted $\mathsf{MIN\ SAT}(\{\mathsf{OR}_{3,1}, \mathsf{F}, \mathsf{T}\})$ A-reduces to Weighted $\mathsf{MIN\ SAT}(\{\mathsf{OR}_{3,2}, \mathsf{F}, \mathsf{T}\})$, which in turn A-reduces to Weighted $\mathsf{MIN\ SAT}(\mathcal{F})$. Weights can be removed as usual using Lemma 7.2.   □

The problem MIN HORN DELETION may be shown to be "hard" to approximate to within a factor of $2^{\log^{1-\epsilon} n}$ by reducing from a variant of the "label cover" problem introduced by [1] (see [55] and the references therein).

Lemma 7.43 *For every $\epsilon > 0$, MIN HORN DELETION is NP-hard to approximate to within a factor of $2^{\log^{1-\epsilon} n}$.*

7.5   The class (Weighted) MIN ONES

Here we prove the following classification theorem for the class MIN ONES.

Theorem 7.44 [MIN ONES classification theorem] [55] *For any constraint set $\mathcal{F}$, the problem (Weighted) MIN ONES$(\mathcal{F})$ is either in PO or APX-complete or NEAREST CODEWORD-complete or MIN HORN DELETION-complete or poly-APX-complete or the decision problem is NP-hard. Furthermore,*

1. *if $\mathcal{F}$ is 0-valid or weakly negative or width-2 affine, then (Weighted) MIN ONES$(\mathcal{F})$ is in PO.*

2. *Else if $\mathcal{F}$ is bijunctive or IHS-B, then (Weighted) MIN ONES$(\mathcal{F})$ is APX-complete.*

3. *Else if $\mathcal{F}$ is affine, then MIN ONES$(\mathcal{F})$ is NEAREST CODEWORD-complete.*

4. *Else if $\mathcal{F}$ is weakly positive, then* (Weighted) MIN ONES$(\mathcal{F})$ *is* MIN HORN DELETION-*complete.*

5. *Else if $\mathcal{F}$ is 1-valid, then* MIN ONES$(\mathcal{F})$ *is* poly-APX-*complete and* Weighted MIN ONES$(\mathcal{F})$ *is decidable but hard to approximate to within any factor.*

6. *Else finding any feasible solution to* (Weighted) MIN ONES$(\mathcal{F})$ *is NP-hard.*

7.5.1 Preliminaries: MIN ONES versus MIN SAT

We start with the following easy relation between MIN SAT and MIN ONES problems. Recall that a family $\mathcal{F}$ is decidable if membership in SAT$(\mathcal{F})$ is decidable in polynomial time.

Proposition 7.45 *For any decidable constraint family $\mathcal{F}$,* Weighted MIN ONES$(\mathcal{F})$ *AP-reduces to* Weighted MIN SAT$(\mathcal{F} \cup \{F\})$.

Proof: Let $\mathcal{I}$ be an instance of Weighted MIN ONES$(\mathcal{F})$ over variables $x_1, \ldots, x_n$ with weights $w_1, \ldots, w_n$. Let $w_{\max}$ be the largest weight. We construct an instance $\mathcal{I}'$ of Weighted MIN SAT$(\mathcal{F} \cup \{F\})$ by leaving the constraints of $\mathcal{I}$ (each with weight $nw_{\max}$), and adding a constraint $F(x_i)$ of weight w_i for any $i = 1, \ldots, n$. Notice that whenever $\mathcal{I}$ is feasible, the optimum value for $\mathcal{I}$ equals the optimum value for $\mathcal{I}'$. Given a r-approximate solution to $\vec{x}$ to $\mathcal{I}'$, we check to see if $\mathcal{I}$ is feasible and if so find any feasible solution $\vec{x}'$ and output solution (from among $\vec{x}$ and $\vec{x}'$) that achieves a lower objective. It is clear that the solution is at least an r-approximate solution if $\mathcal{I}$ is feasible. $\qquad\square$

Reducing a MIN SAT problem to a MIN ONES problem is slightly less general.

Proposition 7.46 *For any function f, let f' and f'' denote the functions $f'(\vec{x}, y) = $ OR$(f(\vec{x}), y)$ and $f''(\vec{x}, y) = $ XOR$(f(\vec{x}), y)$, respectively. If constraint families $\mathcal{F}$ and $\mathcal{F}'$ are such that for every $f \in \mathcal{F}$, f' or f'' is in $\mathcal{F}'$, then* Weighted MIN SAT$(\mathcal{F})$ *AP-reduces to* Weighted MIN ONES$(\mathcal{F}')$.

Proof: Given an instance $\mathcal{I}$ of Weighted MIN SAT$(\mathcal{F})$ we create an instance $\mathcal{I}'$ of Weighted MIN ONES$(\mathcal{F}')$ as follows: For every constraint C_j we introduce an auxiliary variable y_j. The variable takes the same weight as the constraint C_j in $\mathcal{I}$. The original variables are retained with weight zero. If the constraint $C_j(\vec{x}) \vee y_j$ is a constraint of $\mathcal{F}'$ we apply that constraint, else we apply the constraint $C_j(\vec{x}) \oplus y = 1$. Given an assignment to the variables of $\mathcal{I}$, notice that by setting $y_j = \neg C_j$, we get a feasible solution to $\mathcal{I}'$ with the same objective value; conversely, a feasible solution to $\mathcal{I}'$ when projected onto the variables $\vec{x}$ gives a solution with the same value to the objective function of $\mathcal{I}$. This shows that the optimum value to $\mathcal{I}'$ equals that of $\mathcal{I}$ and that an r-approximate solution to $\mathcal{I}'$ projects to give an r-approximate solution to $\mathcal{I}$. $\qquad\square$

Finally the following easy proposition is invoked at a few places.

Proposition 7.47 *If $\mathcal{F}$ implements f, then $\mathcal{F}^-$ implements f^-.*

7.5.2 Containment results for MIN ONES

Lemma 7.48 [PO containment] *If $\mathcal{F}$ is 0-valid or 1-valid or affine with width two, then* Weighted MIN ONES$(\mathcal{F})$ *is solvable exactly in polynomial time.*

Proof: Follows from Lemma 7.13 and from the observation that for any family $\mathcal{F}$, solving Weighted MIN ONES($\mathcal{F}$) to optimality reduces to solving Weighted MAX ONES($\mathcal{F}^-$) to optimality.   □

Lemma 7.49 [APX containment] *If $\mathcal{F}$ is bijunctive or IHS-B, then* Weighted MIN ONES($\mathcal{F}$) *is in* APX.

Proof: For the case when $\mathcal{F}$ is bijunctive, a 2-approximate algorithm is given by Hochbaum et al. [38].

Consider now the case when $\mathcal{F}$ *is IHS-B*. Here it suffices to consider the case where $\mathcal{F}$ is IHS-$B+$, since if $\mathcal{F}$ is IHS-$B-$, then it is weakly negative, and by Lemma 7.48 exact solutions can be found in polynomial time. By Proposition 5.40 it is sufficient to consider only basic IHS-B+ constraints. We use linear-programming relaxations and deterministic rounding. Letting k be the maximum arity of a function in $\mathcal{F}$, we will give a k-approximate algorithm. Let $\phi = \{C_1, \ldots, C_m\}$ be an instance of Weighted MIN ONES($\mathcal{F}$) over variable set $X = \{x_1, \ldots, x_n\}$ with weights $w_1, \ldots, w_n$. The following is an integer linear programming formulation of finding the minimum weight satisfying assignment for ϕ.

$$
\begin{aligned}
\text{Minimize} \quad & \sum_i w_i y_i \\
\text{Subject to} \quad & \\
& y_{i_1} + \cdots + y_{i_h} \geq 1 \quad \forall (x_{i_1} \vee \cdots \vee x_{i_h}) \in \phi \\
& y_{i_1} - y_{i_2} \geq 0 \quad \forall (x_{i_1} \vee \bar{x}_{i_2}) \in \phi \qquad \text{(SCB)} \\
& y_i = 0 \quad \forall \bar{x}_i \in \phi \\
& y_i = 1 \quad \forall x_i \in \phi \\
& y_i \in \{0,1\} \quad \forall i \in \{1, \ldots, n\}.
\end{aligned}
$$

Consider now the linear programming relaxation obtained by relaxing the $y_i \in \{0,1\}$ constraints into $0 \leq y_i \leq 1$. We first find an optimum solution $\mathbf{y}^*$ for the relaxation and then we define a 0/1 solution by setting $y_i = 0$ if $y_i^* < 1/k$, and $y_i = 1$ if $y_i^* \geq 1/k$. It is easy to see that this rounding increases the cost of the solution at most k times and that the obtained solution is feasible for (SCB).   □

Lemma 7.50 [NEAREST CODEWORD containment] *For any affine family $\mathcal{F}$, the problem* Weighted MIN ONES($\mathcal{F}$) *is A-reducible to* NEAREST CODEWORD.

Proof: From Lemmas 7.33 and 5.20 we have that Weighted MIN ONES($\mathcal{F}$) is A-reducible to Weighted MIN ONES($\{\text{XNOR}_3, \text{XOR}_3\}$). From Proposition 7.45, we have that Weighted MIN ONES($\{\text{XNOR}_3, \text{XOR}_3\}$) A-reduces to Weighted MIN SAT($\{\text{XOR}_3, \text{XNOR}_3, F\}$). Notice further that the family $\{\text{XNOR}_3, \text{XOR}_3\}$ can implement F (by Lemma 5.25). Thus we have that Weighted MIN ONES($\mathcal{F}$) A-reduces to Weighted MIN SAT($\{\text{XOR}_3, \text{XNOR}_3, \}$), which is the NEAREST CODEWORD problem.   □

Lemma 7.51 [MIN HORN DELETION containment] *For any weakly positive family $\mathcal{F}$,* Weighted MIN ONES($\mathcal{F}$) *A-reduces to* MIN HORN DELETION.

Proof: The proof follows from the following sequence of assertions:

1. $\{\text{OR}_{3,1}, \text{F}, \text{T}\}$ perfectly implements $\mathcal{F}$ (Lemma 7.34).

2. Weighted MIN ONES($\mathcal{F}$) A-reduces to Weighted MIN ONES($\{\text{OR}_{3,1}, \text{F}, \text{T}\}$) (Lemma 5.20).

3. Weighted MIN ONES($\{OR_{3,1}, F, T\}$) AP-reduces to Weighted MIN SAT($\{OR_{3,1}, F, T\}$) = MIN HORN DELETION (Proposition 7.45). □

Proposition 7.52 [poly-APX containment] *If $\mathcal{F}$ is decidable, then* MIN ONES($\mathcal{F}$) *is in* poly-APX.

Proof: The proposition follows immediately from the fact that in this case it is easy to determine if the input instance is feasible and if so, if the optimum value is zero. If so we output the $\vec{0}$ as the solution, else we output any feasible solution. Since the objective is at least 1 and the solution has value at most n, this is an n-approximate solution. □

7.5.3 Hardness results for MIN ONES

We start by considering the hardest problems first. The case when $\mathcal{F}$ is not decidable is immediate. We move to the case where $\mathcal{F}$ may be 1-valid, but not in any other of Schaefer's easy classes.

Lemma 7.53 [poly-APX-hardness] *If $\mathcal{F}$ is not 0-valid or bijunctive or affine or weakly positive or weakly negative, then* Weighted MIN ONES($\mathcal{F}$) *is hard to approximate to within any factor, and* MIN ONES($\mathcal{F}$) *is* poly-APX-*hard.*

Proof: We first show how to handle the weighted case. The hardness for the unweighted case will follow easily. Consider a function $f \in \mathcal{F}$ which is not weakly positive. For such an f, there exists assignments $\vec{a}$ and $\vec{b}$ such that $f(\vec{a}) = 1$ and $f(\vec{b}) = 0$ and $\vec{a}$ is zero in every coordinate where $\vec{b}$ is zero. (Such an input pair exists for every non-monotone function f and every monotone function is also weakly positive.) Now let f' be the constraint obtained from f by restricting it to inputs where $\vec{b}$ is one and setting all other inputs to zero. Then f' is a satisfiable function which is not 1-valid. We can now apply Schaefer's theorem [82] to conclude that SAT($\mathcal{F} \cup \{f'\}$) is hard to decide. We now reduce an instance of deciding SAT($\mathcal{F} \cup \{f'\}$) to approximating Weighted MIN ONES($\mathcal{F}$). Given an instance $\mathcal{I}$ of SAT($\mathcal{F} \cup \{f'\}$), we create an instance which has some auxiliary variables $W_1, \ldots, W_k$ which are all supposed to take on the value zero. This in enforced by giving them very large weights. We now replace every occurrence of the constraint f' in $\mathcal{I}$ by the constraint f on the corresponding variables with the W_i's in places which were set to zero in f to obtain f'. It is clear that if a "small" weight solution exists to the resulting Weighted MIN ONES($\mathcal{F}$) problem, then $\mathcal{I}$ is satisfiable, else it is not. Thus we conclude it is NP-hard to approximate Weighted MIN ONES($\mathcal{F}$) to within any bounded factors.

For the unweighted case, it suffices to observe that by using polynomially bounded weights above, we get a poly-APX-hardness. Further, one can get rid of weights entirely by replicating variables. □

We may now restrict our attention to function families $\mathcal{F}$ that are 2CNF or affine or weakly positive or weakly negative or 0-valid. In particular, by the containment results shown in the previous section, in all such cases the problem Weighted MIN ONES($\mathcal{F}$) is in poly-APX. We now give a weight-removing lemma which allow us to focus on showing the hardness of the weighted problems.

Lemma 7.54 *If $\mathcal{F}$ is bijunctive or affine or weakly positive or weakly negative or 0-valid, then* Weighted MIN ONES($\mathcal{F}$) *AP-reduces to* MIN ONES($\mathcal{F}$).

Proof: By Lemma 7.2 it suffices to verify that Weighted MIN ONES($\mathcal{F}$) is in poly-APX in all cases. If $\mathcal{F}$ is weakly negative or 0-valid, then this follows from Lemma 7.48. If $\mathcal{F}$ is bijunctive then this follows from Lemma 7.49. If $\mathcal{F}$ is affine or weakly positive, then it A-reduces to NEAREST CODEWORD or MIN HORN DELETION respectively which are in poly-APX by Corollary 7.35. □

Before dealing with the remaining cases, we prove one more lemma that is useful in dealing with MIN ONES problems.

Lemma 7.55 *For every constraint set $\mathcal{F}$ such that $\mathcal{F} \cup \{F\}$ is decidable,* Weighted MIN ONES($\mathcal{F} \cup \{F\}$) *AP-reduces to* Weighted MIN ONES($\mathcal{F}$).

Proof: Given an instance $\mathcal{I}$ of Weighted MIN ONES($\mathcal{F}\cup\{F\}$) on n variables $x_1, \ldots, x_n$ with weights $w_1, \ldots, w_n$, we create an instance $\mathcal{I}'$ of Weighted MIN ONES($\mathcal{F}$), on the variables $x_1, \ldots, x_n$ using all the constraints of $\mathcal{I}$ that are from $\mathcal{F}$; and for every variable x_i such that $F(x_i)$ is a constraint of $\mathcal{I}$, we increase the weight of the variable x_i to $nw_{\max}$, where $w_{\max}$ is the maximum of the weights $w_1, \ldots, w_n$. As in Lemma 7.45, we observe that if $\mathcal{I}$ is feasible, then the optima for $\mathcal{I}$ and $\mathcal{I}'$ are equal; and given an r-approximate solution to $\mathcal{I}'$, we can find an r-approximate solution to $\mathcal{I}$. Furthermore, since $\mathcal{F} \cup \{F\}$ is decidable, we can decide whether or not $\mathcal{I}$ is feasible. □

We now deal with the affine problems.

Lemma 7.56 [NEAREST CODEWORD-hardness] *If $\mathcal{F}$ is affine but not width-2 affine or 0-valid, then* MIN ONES(XOR_3) *is AP-reducible to* Weighted MIN ONES($\mathcal{F}$).

Proof: Notice that since $\mathcal{F}$ is affine, so is $\mathcal{F}^-$. Furthermore, $\mathcal{F}^-$ is neither width-2 affine nor 1-valid. Thus, by Lemma 7.17, $\mathcal{F}^-$ perfectly implements either the family $\{\text{XNOR}_3\}$ or the family $\{\text{XOR}, \text{XNOR}_4\}$. Thus, by applying Proposition 7.47, we get that $\mathcal{F}$ implements either XOR_3 or the family $\{\text{XOR}, \text{XNOR}_4\}$. In the former case, we are done (by Lemma 5.20). In the latter case, notice that the constraints $\text{XNOR}_4(x_1, x_2, x_3, x_5)$ and $\text{XOR}(x_4, x_5)$ perfectly implement the constraint $\text{XOR}_4(x_1, x_2, x_3, x_5)$. Thus we conclude that Weighted MIN ONES(XOR_4) is AP-reducible to Weighted MIN ONES($\mathcal{F}$). Finally we use Lemma 7.55 to conclude that the family Weighted MIN ONES($\{\text{XOR}, F\}$) is AP-reducible to Weighted MIN ONES($\mathcal{F}$). The lemma follows from the fact that $\text{XOR}_3(x_1, x_2, x_3)$ is perfectly implemented by the constraints $\text{XOR}_4(x_1, x_2, x_3, x_4)$ and $F(x_4)$. □

Lemma 7.57 *If $\mathcal{F}$ is affine but not width-2 affine or 0-valid, then, for every $\epsilon > 0$,* MIN ONES($\mathcal{F}$) *is* NEAREST CODEWORD-*hard and hard to approximate to within a factor of $\Omega(2^{\log^{1-\epsilon} n})$.*

Proof: The proof follows from the following sequence of reductions:

NEAREST CODEWORD

$=$ Weighted MIN SAT($\{\text{XOR}_3, \text{XNOR}_3\}$)

$\leq_{\text{AP}}$ Weighted MIN ONES($\{\text{XOR}_4, \text{XNOR}_4\}$) (using Proposition 7.46)

$\leq_{\text{AP}}$ Weighted MIN ONES($\{\text{XOR}_3, \text{XOR}\}$) (see below)

$\leq_{\text{AP}}$ Weighted MIN ONES(XOR_3) (using Lemma 7.55)

$\leq_{\text{AP}}$ Weighted MIN ONES($\mathcal{F}$) (using Lemmas 7.56 and 5.20)

$\leq_{\text{AP}}$ MIN ONES($\mathcal{F}$) (using Lemma 7.54).

The second reduction above follows by combining Lemma 5.20 with the observation that the family $\{\mathsf{XOR}_3, \mathsf{XOR}\}$ perfectly implements the functions XOR_4 and XNOR_4 as shown next. The constraints $\mathsf{XOR}_3(u,v,w)$ and $\mathsf{XOR}_3(w,x,y)$ perfectly implement the constraint $\mathsf{XNOR}_4(u,v,x,y)$; the constraints $\mathsf{XOR}_4(u,v,w,x)$ and $\mathsf{XOR}(w,y)$ perfectly implement $\mathsf{XOR}_4(u,v,x,y)$. The hardness of approximation of NEAREST CODEWORD follows from Lemma 7.40.   □

Lemma 7.58 [MIN HORN DELETION-hardness] *If $\mathcal{F}$ is weakly positive but not IHS-B or 0-valid, then* MIN ONES$(\mathcal{F})$ *is* MIN HORN DELETION-*hard, and hence hard to approximate within $2^{\log^{1-\epsilon} n}$ for any $\epsilon > 0$.*

Proof: Notice that in this case we know that $\mathcal{F} \cup \{\mathsf{T}, \mathsf{F}\}$ perfectly implements $\mathsf{OR}_{3,1}$. The lemma now follows from the following sequence of reductions:

MIN HORN DELETION

$\quad = \quad$ Weighted MIN SAT($\{\mathsf{OR}_{3,1}, \mathsf{T}, \mathsf{F}\}$

$\quad \leq_{\mathrm{AP}} \quad$ Weighted MIN ONES($\{\mathsf{OR}_{4,1}, \mathsf{OR}_2, \mathsf{OR}_{2,1}\}$) (using Proposition 7.46)

$\quad \leq_{\mathrm{AP}} \quad$ Weighted MIN ONES($\{\mathsf{OR}_{3,1}, \mathsf{T}, \mathsf{F}\}$) (using Lemmas 7.34 and 5.20)

$\quad \leq_{\mathrm{AP}} \quad$ Weighted MIN ONES($\mathcal{F} \cup \{\mathsf{T}, \mathsf{F}\}$) (using Lemmas 5.27 and 5.20)

$\quad \leq_{\mathrm{AP}} \quad$ Weighted MIN ONES($\mathcal{F} \cup \{\mathsf{F}\}$) (using Lemma 5.24, part 2, to

$\qquad\qquad\qquad\qquad\qquad\qquad\qquad\qquad$ perfectly implement T)

$\quad \leq_{\mathrm{AP}} \quad$ Weighted MIN ONES($\mathcal{F}$) (using Lemma 7.55)

$\quad \leq_{\mathrm{AP}} \quad$ MIN ONES($\mathcal{F}$) (using Lemma 7.2).

The hardness of approximation follows from Lemma 7.43.   □

Lemma 7.59 MIN ONES(OR_0) *is APX-hard.*

Proof: We reduce MIN VERTEX COVER to MIN ONES(OR_0). Given a graph G on n vertices, we construct an instance of MIN ONES(OR_0) on n variables $x_1, \ldots, x_n$. For every edge between vertex i and j of G, we create a constraint $\mathsf{OR}_0(x_i, x_j)$. We notice that there is a one-to-one correspondence between an assignment to the variables and vertex covers in G (with variables assigned 1 corresponding to vertices in the cover) and the minimum vertex cover minimizes the sum of the variables. The lemma follows from the fact that MIN VERTEX COVER is APX-hard [74, 3].   □

Lemma 7.60 [APX-hardness] *If $\mathcal{F}$ is not 0-valid, or weakly negative or affine with width 2, then* MIN ONES$(\mathcal{F})$ *is APX-hard.*

Proof: We first make some simplifying observations. First, we can assume $\mathcal{F}$ is not affine, since the case when $\mathcal{F}$ was affine was shown to be NEAREST CODEWORD-hard in Lemma 7.57. By Lemma 7.2 it suffices to show that Weighted MIN ONES$(\mathcal{F})$ is APX-hard. By Lemma 7.55 it suffices to show that Weighted MIN ONES$(\mathcal{F} \cup \{\mathsf{F}\})$ is APX-hard. Since $\mathcal{F} \cup \{\mathsf{F}\}$ is not 0-valid or 1-valid or C-closed it implements every function in $\mathcal{F} \cup \{\mathsf{F}, \mathsf{T}\}$ (by part 2 of Lemma 5.24). Thus it suffices to show APX-hardness of Weighted MIN ONES$(\mathcal{F} \cup \{\mathsf{F}, \mathsf{T}\})$ for a non-affine and non-weakly-negative family $\mathcal{F}$. In turn it suffices to show that $\mathcal{F} \cup \{\mathsf{F}, \mathsf{T}\}$ perfectly implements the function OR_0.

Using the fact that $\mathcal{F}$ is not weakly negative (and applying Lemma 5.26) we have that $\mathcal{F} \cup \{\mathsf{F}, \mathsf{T}\}$ perfectly implements either OR_0 or XOR. In the former case, we are done. In the latter case, we use the fact that $\mathcal{F}$ is not affine to get a perfect implementation of one of the functions $\mathsf{OR}_0, \mathsf{OR}_1$ or OR_2. Combined with the XOR function, any of these functions gives a perfect implementation of the function OR_0. $\qquad\square$

Chapter 8

Input-Restricted Constrained Satisfaction Problems

So far we have seen that for NP-hard optimization problems in our framework even the goal of finding near-optimal solutions turns out to be intractable. In particular, any optimization problem that is not in PO turns out to be at least APX-hard. An interesting question is whether there are restricted versions of our optimization problems that are hard to solve optimally and "easy" to approximate — a notion that we formalize by the existence of polynomial time approximation schemes (PTAS). One natural way of creating a restricted version of a problem is to limit its space of input instances. In this chapter, we study two widely different input restrictions for optimization problems. These restrictions are mutually exclusive and for each one of them we will show that the restricted classes of optimization problems contain many NP-hard problems that exhibit a PTAS.

The first restriction that we study is expressed in terms of the graph-theoretic property of *planarity*. At first glance, our input instances do not appear to have any graph-theoretic structure. But as it turns out, there is a natural way of associating a graph with each input instance. Informally, the graph contains a vertex for each constraint application and each variable, and there is an edge between a "variable" vertex and a "constraint" vertex if the constraint contains the variable. We will study the behavior of our optimization problems restricted to input instances with planar associated graphs. While the planarity restriction strongly constrains the interaction between various constraint applications, somewhat surprisingly, one can show the classification theorem for SAT problems largely remains unaltered under this restriction. We will identify broad subclasses of planar input-restricted problems that exhibit a PTAS.

The second input-restriction that we study is referred to as the *density* restriction. We say that an $\mathcal{F}$-collection of constraint applications on n variables is dense if it contains essentially a largest number possible (modulo constant factors) of constraint applications for the family $\mathcal{F}$. The density restriction is in strong contrast to the planarity restriction above in that it seems to enforce a strong interaction between constraint applications.

8.1 The planarity restriction

In order to formally define planar input-restricted instances of constraint satisfaction problems, we introduce the notion of an *incidence graph*.

Definition 8.1 [incidence graph]   *Let $\mathcal{C}$ be a collection of constraint applications f_1, $f_2, \ldots, f_m$ defined over n variables $x_1, x_2, \ldots, x_n$. Then,* the incidence graph *of $\mathcal{C}$ is an undirected graph $G = (V, E)$, defined as follows:*

- *V contains a vertex F_i for each constraint application f_i and a vertex X_j for each variable x_j, and*

- *E contains an edge (F_i, X_j) whenever the variable x_j occurs in the constraint application f_i.*

An input instance $\mathcal{C}$ is called *planar* if the incidence graph of $\mathcal{C}$ is planar. Let $\mathcal{S}$ be one of the classes SAT, MAX SAT, MAX ONES, MIN ONES or MIN SAT. Then Planar $\mathcal{S}$ refers to the class $\mathcal{S}$ with input restricted to instances with planar incidence graphs. We start by showing that the planarity restriction does not seem to significantly alter the complexity of decision problems. In particular, we can adapt the proof of Theorem 6.2 to obtain the following analogue for Planar SAT$(\mathcal{F})$.

Theorem 8.2 *For any constraint family $\mathcal{F}$, if SAT$(\mathcal{F})$ is NP-complete, then Planar SAT$(\mathcal{F} \cup \{\mathsf{F}, \mathsf{T}\})$ is NP-complete as well. Furthermore, if $\mathcal{F}$ is non-C-closed, then Planar SAT$(\mathcal{F})$ is NP-complete whenever SAT$(\mathcal{F})$ is NP-complete.*

Proof: Let $\mathcal{F}$ be a constraint family such that SAT$(\mathcal{F})$ is NP-complete. Then by Lemma 6.3, we know that SAT$(\{\mathsf{One\_in\_Three}\})$ can be reduced to SAT$(\mathcal{F} \cup \{\mathsf{F}, \mathsf{T}\})$. It is known that Planar SAT$(\{\mathsf{One\_in\_Three}\})$ is NP-complete [26]. Thus, to prove the first part of the theorem, it suffices to show that the reduction given by Lemma 6.3 is planarity preserving. Since the reduction simply replaces each constraint application of the form $\mathsf{One\_in\_Three}(x, y, z)$ with a $(\mathcal{F} \cup \{\mathsf{F}, \mathsf{T}\})$-collection of constraint applications, it suffices to prove that the incidence graph of this implementation has a planar embedding with all three variables x, y and z on the outer face. Since our implementation is built by composing a series of implementations, this property needs to be verified for the entire sequence of implementations. This can be done in a straightforward manner, but the details are tedious and we omit them here.

Similarly, the second part of the theorem follows from an easy verification of the fact that any non-C-closed family $\mathcal{F}$ can perfectly implement the constraints F and T (Lemma 5.24) in a planarity-preserving manner. $\square$

8.1.1 Planarity and approximability

It is clear from Theorem 8.2 that planar restrictions of the classes MAX SAT, MAX ONES, MIN ONES and MIN SAT continue to capture NP-hard optimization problems. Planar restriction of these classes contain many fundamental NP-hard optimization problems, including Planar MAX 3-SAT [66], Planar MAX INDEPENDENT SET [33], and Planar MIN VERTEX COVER [66]. We now identify conditions under which the planar input-restricted problems exhibit a PTAS. We start with a definition.

Definition 8.3 [monotone/anti-monotone constraints] *A constraint function f is called* monotone (anti-monotone) *if f can be expressed by a Boolean formula that contains only positive (negative) literals.*

A constraint set $\mathcal{F}$ is *monotone* (*anti-monotone*) if every $f \in \mathcal{F}$ is monotone (anti-monotone). The main result of this section is as follows.

Theorem 8.4 [41, 53] *For any constraint family $\mathcal{F}$,* Planar MAX SAT($\mathcal{F}$) *is in* PTAS. *For any anti-monotone $\mathcal{F}$,* Planar MAX ONES($\mathcal{F}$) *is in* PTAS. *For any monotone $\mathcal{F}$,* Planar MIN ONES($\mathcal{F}$) *is in* PTAS.

Observe that Planar MAX ONES confined only to anti-monotone constraint families captures the NP-hard problem Planar MAX INDEPENDENT SET, and similarly, Planar MIN ONES confined only to anti-monotone constraint families captures the NP-hard problem Planar MIN VERTEX COVER. Thus Planar MAX INDEPENDENT SET and Planar VERTEX COVER all have a PTAS. Notice that we do not indicate any PTAS results for the class Planar MIN SAT. This is essentially explained by Theorem 8.2 which suggests that the dichotomy of the class SAT is largely preserved under the planarity restriction.

Theorem 8.4 is not surprising since it is well-known that many graph optimization problems that are hard to approximate on general instances become significantly easier to approximate on planar graphs. Lipton and Tarjan [68, 69] were the first to present a PTAS for an NP-hard optimization problem on planar graphs; namely, maximum independent sets in planar graphs. Subsequently, Chiba, Nishizeki, and Saito [13] extended this to find a maximum induced subgraph satisfying a hereditary property determined by connected components. Soon after, in a remarkable paper Baker [6] developed a powerful technique to obtain a PTAS for a surprisingly large number of NP-hard graph optimization problems. The proof of Theorem 8.4 builds on Baker's technique. In what follows, we start with an overview of Baker's approach in Section 8.1.2. Then in Sections 8.1.3 and 8.1.4, we establish the PTAS results for each of Planar MAX SAT, Planar MAX ONES and Planar MIN ONES.

8.1.2 An overview of Baker's technique

We start by defining a subclass of planar graphs that plays a central role in Baker's approach.

Definition 8.5 [*p*-Outerplanar Graph] *A 1-outerplanar graph, or simply an outerplanar graph, is a planar graph that has an embedding in the plane with all vertices appearing on the outer face. A p-outerplanar graph is a planar graph that has an embedding in the plane in which deleting all vertices on the outer face yields a $(p-1)$-outerplanar graph.*

A useful structural property of outerplanar graphs is as follows.

Lemma 8.6 [8, 9] *A p-outerplanar graph has a balanced separator[5] of size at most $3p - 1$. Moreover, for any constant p, such a balanced separator can be found by a linear time algorithm.*

Baker [6] observed that many NP-hard optimization problems can be solved optimally in polynomial time on $O(1)$-outerplanar graphs. Furthermore, it was observed that for many such problems, a planar instance can be *approximately* reduced to a polynomial-sized collection of *p*-outerplanar instances for some constant *p*. Thus an approximate solution to the original instance can be put together by optimally solving the collection of $O(1)$-outerplanar instances. We will show that this basic paradigm can be applied to problems in our optimization classes as well.

---

[5] A *balanced separator* for a graph $G = (V, E)$ is any set $X \subset V$ such that the graph induced by deleting the vertices in X has no component of size larger than $2|V|/3$.

8.1.3   Planar MAX SAT

We begin by designing a polynomial time algorithm to compute optimal solutions when the
input belongs to the class p-Outerplanar MAX SAT$(\mathcal{F})$ for some constant p. Let k denote
the maximum arity of a constraint in $\mathcal{F}$ and let G denote the incidence graph of a given
input instance. The first step is to find a separator S of size at most $3p - 1$ for G. The set
S consists of variable vertices as well as the constraint vertices, and its removal partitions
G into two subgraphs G_1 and G_2. Let $V(S)$ denote the set of all variables that are either
directly present in S or occur in some constraint that is present in S. We now use a dynamic
programming approach as follows.

- Fix a guess $\vec{g}$ of values for the variables in $V(S)$. Let $X[\vec{g}]$ denote the set of constraints
  in G that are satisfied by the guess $\vec{g}$ and let $Y[\vec{g}]$ denote the set of constraints in G that
  are set to false by the guess $\vec{g}$.

- Remove all vertices in the sets $V(S)$, $X[\vec{g}]$ and $Y[\vec{g}]$ from each of G_1 and G_2, and let
  the resulting graphs be $G_1[\vec{g}]$ and $G_2[\vec{g}]$, respectively.

- Recursively compute the optimum values for each of $G_1[\vec{g}]$ and $G_2[\vec{g}]$.

- The optimum value OPT(G) is given by the guess $\vec{g}$ that maximizes the following sum:
  $X[\vec{g}] + \text{OPT}(G_1[\vec{g}]) + \text{OPT}(G_2[\vec{g}])$.

Observe that since $|V(S)| \leq k(3p - 1)$, the number of guesses tried above is at most
$2^{k(3p-1)}$ which is a constant. Thus if we denote by N the number of vertices in the graph
G, the running time of the above procedure is easily verified to be $N^{2^{O(kp)}} = N^{O(1)}$.

Lemma 8.7 *For any $\mathcal{F}$, $O(1)$-Outerplanar MAX SAT$(\mathcal{F})$ is contained in* P.

We now show that the above result can be used to construct a PTAS for Planar MAX SAT$(\mathcal{F})$.

Theorem 8.8 *For any $\mathcal{F}$, Planar MAX SAT$(\mathcal{F})$ is in* PTAS.

Proof: Let G denote the incidence graph of a given input instance. We show that for any
fixed $\varepsilon > 0$, we can find in polynomial time a solution whose value is at least $(1-\varepsilon)\text{OPT}(G)$.

Assume that the incidence graph G is t-outerplanar for $t \leq n+m$, where n is the number
of variables and m is the number of constraints in the input. Divide the vertices into t levels,
called $L_1, \ldots, L_t$, such that L_t corresponds to the outer face and each level L_i is the outer
face obtained by removing the levels $L_t, \ldots, L_{i+1}$.

Fix any optimal truth assignment, and let s_i denote the *weight of the constraints satisfied*
in level L_i by this assignment. Partition the levels $L_1, \ldots, L_t$ into $p + 1$ groups, $S_0, \ldots, S_p$,
where group S_r is the union of the levels L_i whose index i is congruent to $3r$, $3r + 1$ or
$3r + 2$ modulo p', where $p' = 3(p + 1)$. The value of p will be specified later. By pigeonhole
principle, there exists a group S_j such that

$$\sum_{L_i \in S_j} s_i \leq \frac{\text{OPT}(G)}{p + 1}.$$

This special group S_j may be identified by trying all possible choices of j and picking the
one which yields the best solution. Having fixed the choice of S_j, delete all vertices in the
levels whose index is congruent to $3j + 1$ modulo p', thereby separating the graph into a
collection of disjoint $(p' - 1)$-outerplanar graphs, say $G_1, G_2, \ldots, G_{t'}$, such that the total
optimal value on this collection is at least $(1 - 1/(p + 1)) \times \text{OPT}(G)$. Choose $p = \lceil 1/\varepsilon - 1 \rceil$
to get the desired result.   □

8.1.4 Planar MAX ONES and Planar MIN ONES

We will follow essentially the same approach as for Planar MAX SAT. The following two lemmas can be established in a manner similar to the proof of Lemma 8.7.

Lemma 8.9 *For any $\mathcal{F}$, $O(1)$-Outerplanar MAX ONES($\mathcal{F}$) and $O(1)$-Outerplanar MIN ONES($\mathcal{F}$) are contained in* P.

We now show how this result can be used to obtain a PTAS for planar instances of MIN ONES($\mathcal{F}$) when $\mathcal{F}$ is monotone.

Theorem 8.10 *For any monotone $\mathcal{F}$,* Planar MIN ONES($\mathcal{F}$) *is in* PTAS.

Proof: As before, assume that the incidence graph G is t-outerplanar for $t \leq n + m$, where n is the number of variables and m is the number of constraints in the input. Divide the vertices into t levels, called $L_1, \ldots, L_t$, such that L_t corresponds to the outer face and each level L_i is the outer face obtained by removing the levels $L_t, \ldots, L_{i+1}$.

Fix any optimal truth assignment, and let t_i denote the weight of the variables set to true among the variables that appear in the constraints at level L_i. Partition the levels $L_1, \ldots, L_t$ into $p + 1$ groups, $S_0, \ldots, S_p$, where group S_r is the union of the levels L_i whose index i is congruent to $2r$ or $2r + 1$ modulo p', where $p' = 2(p + 1)$. The value of p will be specified later. By pigeonhole principle, there exists a group S_j such that

$$\sum_{L_i \in S_j} t_i \leq \frac{\text{OPT}(G)}{(p + 1)}.$$

This special group S_j may be identified by trying all possible choices of j and picking the one which yields the best solution. Having fixed the choice of S_j, delete all the constraint vertices in the levels represented in S_j. This separates G into a collection of disjoint $2p$-outerplanar graphs, say $G_1, G_2, \ldots, G_{t'}$, such that $\sum_{i=1}^{t'} \text{OPT}(G_i) \leq \text{OPT}(G)$. Let $\vec{s}$ denote the assignment to the variables as determined by the union of these solutions (note that G_i's partition the variables).

But the solution found above needs to be extended to satisfy the constraints in the layers of the group S_j as well. To do so, we simply find an optimal solution that satisfies the constraints in the layers in S_j. Let $\vec{s'}$ denote the assignment to variables in this solution. By our choice of S_j, the weight of this solution is no more than $\text{OPT}(G)/(p + 1)$. We now combine the assignments for $\vec{s}$ and $\vec{s'}$ into a single assignment as follows: set any variable to true if it is set to true in either $\vec{s}$ or $\vec{s'}$. Since $\mathcal{F}$ is monotone, this modification cannot unsatisfy a previously satisfied constraint. Moreover, the weight of the new solution is at most $(1 + 1/(p + 1))\text{OPT}(G)$. Choose $p = \lceil 1/\varepsilon - 1 \rceil$ to get a $(1 + \varepsilon)$-approximation. $\square$

The proof of the following theorem is similar to the above proof and is hence omitted.

Theorem 8.11 *For any anti-monotone $\mathcal{F}$,* Planar MAX ONES($\mathcal{F}$) *is in* PTAS.

8.2 The density restriction

We now focus on another natural restriction, namely, density. The notion of dense instances is formalized as follows.

Definition 8.12 [dense instance] *Let $\mathcal{C}$ be a collection of m constraint applications defined over n variables, and let k be the largest arity of any constraint in $\mathcal{F}$. Then we say that $\mathcal{C}$ is a* dense *instance if $m = \Omega(n^k)$.*

For any $\mathcal{F}$, we refer to as Dense SAT($\mathcal{F}$) and Dense MAX SAT($\mathcal{F}$) the problems SAT($\mathcal{F}$) and MAX SAT($\mathcal{F}$) with input restricted to dense instances. We now show that the density restriction does not alter the complexity of the underlying decision problems.

Theorem 8.13 *For any constraint set $\mathcal{F}$, SAT($\mathcal{F}$) is NP-complete if and only if* Dense SAT($\mathcal{F}$) *is NP-complete.*

Proof: Let $\mathcal{C}$ be an $\mathcal{F}$-collection of m constraint applications on variables $\vec{x} = \{x_1, \ldots, x_n\}$. Construct a dummy $\mathcal{F}$-collection of constraints $\mathcal{C}'$, which is both dense and satisfiable, as follows. Let $\vec{x}' = \{x_1', \ldots, x_n'\}$ be a set of n new variables and let f be a constraint of largest arity in $\mathcal{F}$. Consider the set of all possible constraint applications constructed by applying f on every k-variable subset of $\vec{x}'$ (there are $\Omega(n^k)$ such constraint applications). By Proposition 5.17 one can find in polynomial time an assignment that satisfies at least $\Omega(n^k)$ constraints in this set. Let $\mathcal{C}'$ be such a collection of satisfiable constraints. Now $\mathcal{C} \cup \mathcal{C}'$ is a dense instance of SAT($\mathcal{F}$) which is satisfiable if and only if $\mathcal{C}$ is satisfiable. Hence Dense SAT($\mathcal{F}$) is NP-complete.   □

The above theorem suggests that our optimization classes contain many problems that remain hard to solve exactly even when restricted to dense instances. However, density does allow for the possibility that a problem may admit a PTAS even if it is hard to solve exactly. For three of the classes, namely MAX ONES, MIN ONES and MIN SAT, even the density condition does not seem to help in getting PTAS. However, for the fourth class, namely, MAX SAT, density does turn out to be very helpful.

We now present our main result here, namely, Dense MAX SAT is contained in PTAS. Arora, Karger, and Karpinski [2] developed a general technique that can be used to find an *additive error* approximation to MAX SAT($\mathcal{F}$). Specifically, for any fixed $\varepsilon > 0$, their technique can be used to find a solution to an instance of MAX SAT($\mathcal{F}$) such that the solution is at most εn^k away from the optimal. On the other hand, according to Proposition 5.17 there exists a solution of value $\Omega(n^k)$ for any dense instance of a MAX SAT($\mathcal{F}$) problem. This latter observation allows one to interpret the additive error approximation scheme of [2] as a *relative error* scheme for dense instances, giving a PTAS for this class of instances.

Definition 8.14 [polynomial integer program (PIP)] *A polynomial integer program refers to an optimization problem of the form:* MAXIMIZE (MINIMIZE) $p(x_1, \ldots, x_n)$ *such that $x_i \in \{0, 1\}$ for $1 \leq i \leq n$; here p is a polynomial. We say that such a program is a (c, d)-PIP if p is a polynomial of degree at most d and each coefficient of a degree i monomial in p is at most cn^{d-i}.*

Even when the parameters c and d are restricted to take only fixed values, (c, d)-PIPs can capture a large variety of NP-hard constraint satisfaction problems. Arora, Karger, and Karpinski [2] showed the following result for approximating (c, d)-PIPs.

Theorem 8.15 [2] *Given a (c, d)-PIP on n variables where c and d are constants, and a fixed $\varepsilon > 0$, there exists a polynomial time algorithm that finds a solution $(x_1^*, \ldots, x_n^*)$ such that $p(x_1^*, \ldots, x_n^*) \geq \text{OPT} - \varepsilon n^d$, where OPT denotes the optimum value of the PIP.*

The idea underlying the above result is an exhaustive sampling technique whereby optimization of a degree d polynomial can be *approximately* reduced to solving an integer linear program. By relaxing the integrality constraints, one can compute in polynomial time an optimal fractional solution to this linear program and then round the fractional solution by the Raghavan and Thompson rounding technique [79]. A detailed exposition of these steps is beyond the scope of this monograph and the reader is referred to [2] for details.

We now show that MAX SAT$(\mathcal{F})$ is closely related to (c, d)-PIPs.

Proposition 8.16 *Let $\mathcal{C}$ be any instance of* MAX SAT$(\mathcal{F})$ *and let k be the largest arity of any constraint in $\mathcal{F}$. Then the problem of finding a solution satisfying a largest number of constraints in $\mathcal{C}$ can be expressed as an instance of $(O(1), k)$-PIP.*

Proof: It follows from the standard arithmetization technique to express $\mathcal{C}$ as a polynomial. $\square$

Combining Theorem 8.15 with Proposition 8.16 above, we get our main result.

Corollary 8.17 *For any $\mathcal{F}$,* Dense MAX SAT$(\mathcal{F})$ *is in* PTAS.

Chapter 9

The Complexity of the Meta-Problems

In the previous chapters we have established classification theorems which identify properties of the constraint sets that determine whether or not a problem is tractable. A natural question is what is the complexity of identifying tractable problems. In other words, how difficult it is to recognize that the problem specified by a given constraint set is indeed tractable. The goal of this chapter is to study this question. Specifically, let $\mathcal{C}$ denote one of the classes SAT, #SAT, QSAT, MAX SAT, MIN SAT, MAX ONES or MIN ONES. We are interested in studying the following *meta-problem*, denoted by Meta-$\mathcal{C}$:

INPUT : A constraint set $\mathcal{F}$.

QUESTION : Is $\mathcal{C}(\mathcal{F})$ in P?

There are many natural ways of specifying a Boolean function, and the complexity of the meta-problem is directly related to the manner that the functions in the input constraint set are specified. We will study the above meta-problem for three natural representations:

- f is specified by its set of satisfying assignments, denoted $\mathtt{sat}(f)$,

- f is specified by a CNF-formula, and

- f is specified by a DNF formula.

We will show that for each of the above representation schemes, either the meta-problem is polynomial time solvable for each one of the classes $\mathcal{C}$ mentioned above, or it is coNP-hard for each class.

9.1 Representation by the set of satisfying assignments

Our main result here is the following theorem.

Theorem 9.1 *For each class $\mathcal{C}$ in our study, the Meta-$\mathcal{C}$ problem is in P if the input constraint set is specified using the set of satisfying assignments representation.*

To establish the above theorem, it suffices to give polynomial time procedures for recognizing the set of properties described in the lemma below.

Lemma 9.2 *Let f be a constraint function specified by its set of satisfying assignments. Then the problem of deciding whether f satisfies any one of the properties below is in* P:

1. *0-valid (1-valid),*

2. *weakly positive (weakly negative),*

3. *affine,*

4. *bijunctive,*

5. *width 2 affine, and*

6. *2-monotone.*

Proof: It is trivial to verify property (1), and for properties (2) through (4), the result easily follows from the characterization of these properties as given in Section 4.4. To verify that the function f of arity k is width 2 affine, we use the following procedure to construct a candidate width 2 affine function $\tilde{f}$ and verify that $\mathtt{sat}(\tilde{f}) = \mathtt{sat}(f)$:

a) Let $x_1, \ldots, x_k$ be the underlying variables.

b) If a variable x_i takes value 1 (0) in each satisfying assignment of f, include the constraint $x_i = 1$ ($x_i = 0$) in $\tilde{f}$.

c) For every pair of variables x_i, x_j such that $x_i = x_j$ in each satisfying assignment, include the constraint $\mathrm{XOR}(x_i, x_j) = 0$ in $\tilde{f}$.

d) Similarly, for every pair of variables x_i, x_j such that $x_i \neq x_j$ in each satisfying assignment, include the constraint $\mathrm{XOR}(x_i, x_j) = 1$ in $\tilde{f}$.

e) Verify that every satisfying assignment of f is also a satisfying assignment for $\tilde{f}$ and that $|\mathtt{sat}(\tilde{f})| = |\mathtt{sat}(f)|$.

It is clear that the above procedure can clearly be implemented in time polynomial in $|\mathtt{sat}(f)|$. We now move to the last property, namely, the property of being a 2-monotone function. We will use the characterization of 2-monotone functions as given by Lemma 4.13. The algorithm below decides in polynomial time whether a constraint f of arity k is 2-monotone. As before, we build a candidate function 2-monotone function $\tilde{f}$ by examining the set of satisfying assignments $\mathtt{sat}(f)$, and verify that $\mathtt{sat}(\tilde{f}) = \mathtt{sat}(f)$.

a) Verify that for each satisfying assignment s, either $Z(s)$ is 0-consistent or $O(s)$ is 1-consistent (both could happen).

b) Let P be the set of assignments s such that $O(s)$ 1-consistent. Let m_1 be the intersection of all these 1-consistent sets.

c) Let Q be the set of assignments such that $Z(s)$ is 0-consistent. Let m_2 be the intersection of all these 0-consistent sets.

d) Let $\tilde{f} = \left(\bigwedge_{x \in m_1} x \right) \vee \left(\bigwedge_{y \in m_2} \bar{y} \right)$. (If f is 2-monotone, then $f \equiv \tilde{f}$.)

e) $|\mathtt{sat}(\tilde{f})| = 2^{k-|m_1|} + 2^{k-|m_2|} - \varepsilon(m_1, m_2)$, where $\varepsilon(m_1, m_2) = 0$ if $m_1 \cap m_2 \neq \emptyset$ and $\varepsilon(m_1, m_2) = 2^{k-|m_1|-|m_2|}$ otherwise.

f) Verify that every satisfying assignment of f is also a satisfying assignment for $\tilde{f}$ and that $|\mathtt{sat}(\tilde{f})| = |\mathtt{sat}(f)|$.   □

9.2   Representation by a CNF-formula

Our main result here is that the Meta-$\mathcal{C}$ problem, for each class $\mathcal{C}$, becomes coNP-hard when the functions are specified by CNF-formulas. Observe that in order to prove this result, it suffices to establish the coNP-hardness of verifying the following three properties:

1. affine,

2. width 2 affine, and

3. 2-monotone.

It is easily seen that together these properties intersect the tractable cases for each one of our classes. We start with properties 1 and 2 above.

Lemma 9.3 *Let f be a constraint function specified as a CNF-formula. Then the problem of deciding whether f is affine (width 2 affine) is* coNP-*hard.*

Proof: We will show that given a CNF-formula f, deciding whether f is logically equivalent to the equation $\alpha = 1$ is coNP-hard. This clearly establishes the claimed result. We will do a reduction from the UNSATISFIABILITY problem defined as below:

INSTANCE : A CNF-formula f.

QUESTION : Is f unsatisfiable?

The UNSATISFIABILITY problem is known to be coNP-complete [14]. Consider an input $f = \bigwedge_{i=1}^{p} C_i$ to the UNSATISFIABILITY problem, where f is defined over a set of variables $\vec{x} = \{x_1, \ldots, x_k\}$. Also, let α be a new variable not in $\vec{x}$. Now consider the formula $f' = \bigwedge_{i=1}^{p}(C_i \vee \alpha)$. It is clear that if f is unsatisfiable, then f' is logically equivalent to the linear system $(\alpha = 1)$ over the field GF(2). Conversely, suppose that f' is logically equivalent to a linear system over the field GF(2). Observe that in this case $|\mathsf{sat}(f')|$ is necessarily a power of 2. By our construction of f', we have $|\mathsf{sat}(f')| = 2^k + |\mathsf{sat}(f)|$, and since $0 \leq |\mathsf{sat}(f)| < 2^k$, $|\mathsf{sat}(f')|$ is a power of 2 if and only if $|\mathsf{sat}(f)| = 0$, that is, if and only if f is unsatisfiable. This completes the proof of the lemma.   □

We next establish coNP-hardness of recognizing 2-monotone functions. We will use the following proposition.

Proposition 9.4 *Given a CNF-formula f, deciding whether f has the all-one assignment as its only satisfying assignment (i.e., $f \equiv (x_1 \wedge \cdots \wedge x_k)$) is* coNP-*hard.*

Proof: We consider the following problem:

INSTANCE : A CNF-formula f.

QUESTION : Is f almost unsatisfiable, that is, f is either unsatisfiable or only satisfied by the all-one assignment?

It is easy to verify that this problem is coNP-complete by using the following reduction from the UNSATISFIABILITY problem. Given an input f to the UNSATISFIABILITY problem, construct the formula $f' = f \wedge (\bar{\alpha})$ (where α is a new variable) as input to the problem above. Clearly, f is unsatisfiable if and only if f' is almost unsatisfiable.

Now let $f = \bigwedge_{i=1}^{p} C_i$ be a CNF-formula, defined over a set of variables $\vec{x} = \{x_1, \ldots, x_k\}$. Consider the formula $f' = \bigwedge_{j=1}^{k} \bigwedge_{i=1}^{p}(C_i \vee x_j)$. It is easy to verify that f is almost unsatisfiable if and only if f' has the all-one assignment as only satisfying assignment. First observe that the all-one assignment, $\vec{1}$, satisfies f'. Also, if f is satisfied by $s \neq \vec{1}$, then f' is also satisfied by s. Conversely, suppose that f is almost unsatisfiable and.that f' is satisfied by $s = (s_1, \ldots, s_k) \neq \vec{1}$. Let j_0 be such that $s_{j_0} = 0$. Since s satisfies f', s satisfies $\bigwedge_{i=1}^{p}(C_i \vee x_{j_0})$. Hence, s satisfies $\bigwedge_{i=1}^{p} C_i = f$, which is a contradiction. $\square$

Lemma 9.5 *Let f be a constraint function specified as a CNF-formula. Then the problem of deciding whether f is 2-monotone is* coNP-*hard.*

Proof: By Proposition 9.4, it is sufficient to show that the problem of deciding whether a CNF-formula has the all-one assignment for only satisfying assignment can be reduced to the problem of deciding whether a CNF-formula defines a 2-monotone function. Given a CNF formula f over a set of variables $\{x_1, \ldots, x_k\}$, we construct a formula f' over the variables $\{x_1, \ldots, x_k\} \cup \{x_1', \ldots, x_k'\} \cup \{\alpha\}$ (where α and $x_i', 1 \leq i \leq k$ are new variables) and defined as follows:

$$f' := f \wedge \bigwedge_{i=1}^{k}(x_i \equiv x_i') \wedge (\alpha).$$

If the all-one assignment is the only satisfying assignment for f, then

$$f' \equiv \bigwedge_{i=1}^{k} x_i \wedge \bigwedge_{i=1}^{k} x_i' \wedge (\alpha);$$

hence, f' is 2-monotone.

Conversely, if f' is 2-monotone then f' is equivalent to a conjunction of positive literals (because of the clause (α)) and this conjunction involves all the variables (because of the clauses $\bigwedge_{i=1}^{k}(x_i \equiv x_i')$). Therefore,

$$f' \equiv \bigwedge_{i=1}^{k} x_i \wedge \bigwedge_{i=1}^{k} x_i' \wedge (\alpha),$$

hence, the all-one assignment is the only satisfying assignment for f. $\square$

We can now conclude the following theorem.

Theorem 9.6 *For each class $\mathcal{C}$ in our study, the* Meta-$\mathcal{C}$ *problem is* coNP-*hard if the input constraint set is specified using the CNF-formula representation.*

9.3   Representation by a DNF-formula

Similar to the case of representation by CNF-formulas, we now show that the Meta-$\mathcal{C}$ problem, for each class $\mathcal{C}$, remains coNP-hard when the functions are specified as DNF-formulas. As before, it suffices to show coNP-hardness of recognizing the properties of being affine, width 2 affine, and 2-monotone. We establish the following analogs of Lemmas 9.3 and 9.5.

Lemma 9.7 *Let f be a constraint function specified as a DNF-formula. Then the problem of deciding whether f is affine (width 2 affine) is* coNP-*hard.*

Proof: The proof is similar to Lemma 9.3. We now provide a reduction from the well-known coNP-complete problem TAUTOLOGY [32, LO8]:

INSTANCE : A DNF-formula f.

QUESTION : Is f satisfied by every assignment?

Given an input f to the **TAUTOLOGY** problem, we create a DNF-formula $f' = f \vee (\alpha)$, where α is a new variable. The claimed result now follows since f is a tautology if and only if f' is logically equivalent to constraint $\alpha = 1$. $\qquad\square$

Lemma 9.8 *Let f be a constraint function specified as a DNF-formula. Then the problem of deciding whether f is 2-monotone is coNP-hard.*

Proof: Once again we use the **TAUTOLOGY** problem as our starting point. Let $f = \bigvee_{i=1}^{p} D_i$ be a DNF-formula, given as input to the **TAUTOLOGY** problem; here each D_i is a conjunction of literals, for $i = 1, \ldots, p$. We construct a DNF-formula f' as below:

$$f' = \bigvee_{i=1}^{p} (D_i \wedge \alpha \wedge \beta) \vee \bigvee_{i=1}^{p} (D_i \wedge \bar{\alpha} \wedge \bar{\beta}),$$

where α and β are new variables. It is easy to verify that f' is 2-monotone if and only if f' is equivalent to $(\alpha \wedge \beta) \vee (\bar{\alpha} \wedge \bar{\beta})$, that is if and only if f is a tautology. This completes the proof. $\qquad\square$

We can now conclude our main result here.

Theorem 9.9 *For each class $\mathcal{C}$ in our study, the* Meta-$\mathcal{C}$ *problem is coNP-hard if the input constraint set is specified using the DNF-formula representation.*

Chapter 10

Concluding Remarks

We have presented a taxonomy of the computational complexity of problems derived from Boolean constraint satisfaction. In the process we have seen some of the central complexity classes such as NP, NC, PSPACE, #P and NPO. When specialized to Boolean constraint satisfaction, these classes partition nicely into just finitely many equivalence classes — where problems within an equivalence class are reducible to one another. A central idea in establishing these partitions is the notion of *implementations*. Implementations allowed us to build in a unified manner a variety of different reductions addressing the varying goals of the decision, counting and optimization problems. The basic toolkit turns out to be significantly more compact than the wide variety of purposes that it is used for.

One of the most significant conclusions we draw from the study of constraint satisfaction problems is that it provides an excellent platform to search for a "formal basis" for "empirical observations". Complexity theory is intended to study the most general forms of computations. However, the generality often poses a barrier when one tries to formalize a noticeable trend among natural problems. Typically, the moment one tries to formalize the trend, a counterexample is found. Usually the counterexample is unnatural, but there is no way to formalize the notion of naturality either! In contrast, specializing classes such as NP, PSPACE and NPO to Boolean constraint satisfaction creates "miniaturized imprints" of these classes that are refined enough to exhibit many phenomena observed in the parent classes and yet coarse enough to preserve such phenomena over all problems contained in them.

Consider for example the unifying notion of reductions used for NP-completeness. Most known reductions are based on "gadgets" — an informal theme that signifies that a combinatorial construct has been used to convert one problem to another. Much of the work towards formally studying gadgets has been confined to specific instances of source and target problems of the reduction (see, for instance, [7]). The finite nature of such problem-specific explorations inherently lacks the ability to highlight any general results that describe the ubiquitous nature of gadget reductions. However, when restricted to constraint satisfaction problems, the elusive notion of a "gadget" reduction can be formalized — it is indeed the notion of reduction via implementations. The results described in the earlier chapters give a very satisfactory explanation of the seemingly universal nature of these reductions.

Constraint satisfaction problems play a particularly significant role in the study of optimization problems. The current decade (1990–2000) has seen an explosion of research studying the approximability of optimization problems. While the research has pointed to significant unifying trends, the trends are sometimes hard to spot from among the natural diversity exhibited by optimization problems; and even when a trend becomes visible, it is hard to formalize or prove it. For example, the classes PO, PTAS, APX, log-APX and poly-APX do seem to be very natural thresholds of approximability with almost all known problems being complete for some of these classes. However, without the use of constraint satisfaction problems, there is no way of formally stating such an assertion. Constraint satisfaction problems actually allow not only a formal assertion, but also give a proof. Several other such trends are described in [56, 55].

In this monograph, we have restricted our attention to cases where complete classification results are known. However, there do exist other complexity classes where a natural restriction to constraint satisfaction may lead to classification results, but such a possibility is either unexamined or has eluded a proof. An example of the former category, i.e., computational tasks where a classification result has not been explored, is the "classical dualization problem" [10, 27, 31]. Here the goal is to find all the minterms of a given generalized satisfiability expression. A wide variety of interesting positive results are known in this case; however, this falls short of classification. It would be interesting to explore this problem further.

A more serious shortcoming of our study is that it has been restricted to the study of constraint satisfaction problems over a Boolean domain. The problems in our framework also extend, quite naturally, to non-Boolean domains. However, the proofs of classification do not, and it is open as to whether the theorems do. Jeavons, Cohen, and Gyssens [44] have brought to the fore the link between the algebraic closure properties of the constraints and the complexity of the corresponding constraint satisfaction problems. Our study motivates this line of research since it appears that when restricted to Boolean domain, algebraic closure properties of the constraints (see Chapter 4, Section 4.4) exactly characterize the complexity of the corresponding constraint satisfaction problems (see Chapter 6). The study of Feder and Vardi [28] already points to some significant technical hurdles in extending the classification results to this domain. However, they also show that classifications of constraint satisfaction problems over non-Boolean domains are of much more than technical interest. It turns out that constraint satisfaction problems over non-Boolean domains are computationally equivalent to problems in "monotone monadic SNP" — a syntactically restricted class of languages within NP, which is, in some sense, the largest class within NP that may show dichotomy results. Their proof of the equivalence between the two classes is highly non-trivial and further motivates the study of constraint satisfaction problems. A complete classification result of all constraint satisfaction problems over arbitrary domains would bring an extemely satisfying conclusion to this line of work, and we look forward to seeing work in this direction.

Bibliography

[1] Sanjeev Arora, László Babai, Jacques Stern, and Z. Sweedyk. The hardness of approximate optima in lattices, codes, and systems of linear equations. *Journal of Computer and System Sciences*, 54(2):317–331, 1997.

[2] Sanjeev Arora, David Karger, and Marek Karpinski. Polynomial time approximation schemes for dense instances of NP-hard problems. *Journal of Computer and System Sciences*, 58(1):193–210, 1999.

[3] Sanjeev Arora, Carsten Lund, Rajeev Motwani, Madhu Sudan, and Mario Szegedy. Proof verification and the hardness of approximation problems. *Journal of the ACM*, 45(3):501–555, 1998.

[4] Sanjeev Arora and Shmuel Safra. Probabilistic checking of proofs: A new characterization of NP. *Journal of the ACM*, 45(1):70–122, 1998.

[5] Bengt Aspvall, Michael F. Plass, and Robert E. Tarjan. A linear-time algorithm for testing the truth of certain quantified Boolean formulas. *Information Processing Letters*, 8(3):121–123, 1979.

[6] Brenda S. Baker. Approximation algorithms for NP-complete problems on planar graphs. *Journal of the ACM*, 41(1):153–180, 1994.

[7] Mihir Bellare, Oded Goldreich, and Madhu Sudan. Free bits, PCPs, and nonapproximability — towards tight results. *SIAM Journal on Computing*, 27(3):804–915, 1998.

[8] Hans L. Bodlaender. Some classes of graphs with bounded treewidth. *Bulletin of the European Association for Theoretical Computer Science*, 36:116–126, 1988.

[9] Hans L. Bodlaender. A linear time algorithm for finding tree-decompositions of small treewidth. In *Proceedings of the Twenty-Fifth Annual ACM Symposium on the Theory of Computing*, pp. 226–234, San Diego, California, 16–18 May 1993.

[10] Endre Boros, Yves Crama, and Peter L. Hammer. Polynomial-time inference of all valid implications for Horn and related formulae. *Annals of Mathematics and Artificial Intelligence*, (1):21–32, 1990.

[11] Endre Boros, Yves Crama, Peter L. Hammer, and Michael E. Saks. A complexity index for satisfiability problems. *SIAM Journal on Computing*, 23(1):45–49, 1994.

[12] Daniel Pierre Bovet and Pierluigi Crescenzi. *Introduction to the Theory of Complexity*. Prentice-Hall, New York, 1993.

[13] Norishige Chiba, Takao Nishizeki, and Nobuji Saito. Applications of the planar separator theorem. *Journal of Information Processing*, 4:203–207, 1981.

[14] Stephen A. Cook. The complexity of theorem-proving procedures. In *Conference Record of Third Annual ACM Symposium on Theory of Computing*, pp. 151–158, Shaker Heights, Ohio, 3–5 May 1971.

[15] Stephen A. Cook. A taxonomy of problems with fast parallel algorithms. *Information and Control*, 64(1-3):2–21, 1985.

[16] Stephen A. Cook and Michael Luby. A simple parallel algorithm for finding a satisfying truth assignment to a 2-CNF formula. *Information Processing Letters*, 27(3):141–145, 1988.

[17] Nadia Creignou. A dichotomy theorem for maximum generalized satisfiability problems. *Journal of Computer and System Sciences*, 51(3):511–522, 1995.

[18] Nadia Creignou and Jean-Jacques Hébrard. On generating all satisfying truth assignments of a generalized CNF-formula. *Theoretical Informatics and Applications*, 31(6):499–511, 1997.

[19] Nadia Creignou and Miki Hermann. Complexity of generalized satisfiability counting problems. *Information and Computation*, 125(1):1–12, 1996.

[20] Pierluigi Crescenzi, Viggo Kann, Riccardo Silvestri, and Luca Trevisan. Structure in approximation classes. *SIAM Journal on Computing*, 28(5):1759–1782, 1999.

[21] Pierluigi Crescenzi and Alessandro Panconesi. Completeness in approximation classes. *Information and Computation*, 93(2):241–262, 1991.

[22] Pierluigi Crescenzi, Riccardo Silvestri, and Luca Trevisan. To weight or not to weight: Where is the question? In *Proceedings of the 4th IEEE Israel Symposium on Theory of Computing and Systems*, pp. 68–77, 1996.

[23] Victor Dalmau. Some dichotomy theorems on constant free Boolean formulas. Tech. report LSI-97-43-R, Departament LSI, Universitat Politècnica de Catalunya, 1997.

[24] Dorit Dor and Michael Tarsi. Graph decomposition is NP-complete: A complete proof of Holyer's conjecture. *SIAM Journal on Computing*, 26(4):1166–1187, 1997.

[25] William F. Dowling and Jean H. Gallier. Linear-time algorithms for testing the satisfiability of propositional Horn formulae. *Journal of Logic Programming*, 1(3):267–284, 1984.

[26] Martin E. Dyer and Alan M. Frieze. Planar 3DM is NP-complete. *Journal of Algorithms*, 7(2):174–184, 1986.

[27] Thomas Eiter and Georg Gottlob. Identifying the minimal transversals of a hypergraph and related problems. *SIAM Journal on Computing*, 24(1):1278–1304, 1995.

[28] Tomás Feder and Moshe Y. Vardi. The computational structure of monotone monadic SNP and constraint satisfaction: A study through datalog and group theory. *SIAM Journal on Computing*, 28(1):57–104, 1998.

[29] Uriel Feige, Shafi Goldwasser, Laszlo Lovász, Shmuel Safra, and Mario Szegedy. Interactive proofs and the hardness of approximating cliques. *Journal of the ACM*, 43(2):268–292, 1996.

[30] Steven Fortune, John Hopcroft, and James Wyllie. The directed subgraph homeomorphism problem. *Theoretical Computer Science*, 10(2):111–121, 1980.

[31] Michael L. Fredman and Leonid Khachiyan. On the complexity of dualization of monotone disjunctive normal forms. *Journal of Algorithms*, 21:618–628, 1996.

[32] Michael R. Garey and David S. Johnson. *Computers and Intractability: A Guide to the Theory of NP-Completeness*. W. H. Freeman and Company, San Francisco, 1979.

[33] Michael R. Garey, David S. Johnson, and Larry J. Stockmeyer. Some simplified NP-complete graph problems. *Theoretical Computer Science*, 1(3):237–267, 1976.

[34] Naveen Garg, Vijay V. Vazirani, and Mihalis Yannakakis. Approximate max-flow min-(multi)cut theorems and their applications. *SIAM Journal on Computing*, 25(2):235–251, 1996.

[35] Leslie M. Goldschlager, Ralph A. Shaw, and John Staples. The maximum flow problem is log space complete for P. *Theoretical Computer Science*, 21(1):105–111, 1982.

[36] Raymond Greenlaw, H. James Hoover, and Walter L. Ruzzo. *Limits to Parallel Computation: P-completeness Theory*. Oxford University Press, 1995.

[37] Pavol Hell and Jaroslav Nešetřil. On the complexity of H-coloring. *Journal of Combinatorial Theory, Series B*, 48(1):92–110, 1990.

[38] Dorit S. Hochbaum, Nimrod Megiddo, Joseph Naor, and Arie Tamir. Tight bounds and 2-approximation algorithms for integer programs with two variables per inequality. *Mathematical Programming Series B*, 62(1):69–83, 1993.

[39] John E. Hopcroft and Jeffrey D. Ullman. *Introduction to Automata Theory, Languages and Computation*. Addison Wesley Publishing Company, Reading, MA, 1979.

[40] A. Horn. On sentences which are true of direct unions of algebras. *Journal of Symbolic Logic*, 16:14–21, 1951.

[41] Harry B. Hunt III, Madhav V. Marathe, Venkatesh Radhakrishnan, S.S. Ravi, Daniel J. Rosenkrantz, and Richard E. Stearns. Approximation schemes using L-reductions. In *Proceedings of the Conference on Foundations of Software Technology and Theoretical Computer Science*, pp. 342–353, 1994.

[42] Harry B. Hunt III, Madhav V. Marathe, Venkatesh Radhakrishnan, and Richard E. Stearns. The complexity of planar counting problems. *SIAM Journal on Computing*, 27(4):1142–1167, 1998.

[43] Brigitte Jaumard and Bruno Simeone. On the complexity of the maximum satisfiability problem for Horn formulas. *Information Processing Letters*, 26(1):1–4, 1987.

[44] Peter Jeavons, David Cohen, and Marc Gyssens. Closure properties of constraints. *Journal of the ACM*, 44(4):527–548, 1997.

[45] David S. Johnson. Approximation algorithms for combinatorial problems. *Journal of Computer and System Sciences*, 9(3):256–278, 1974.

[46] David S. Johnson. A catalog of complexity classes. In J. van Leeuwen, editor, *Handbook of Theoretical Computer Science, Volume A: Algorithms and Complexity*, pp. 67–161. North-Holland, Amsterdam, 1990.

[47] David S. Johnson, Mihalis Yannakakis, and Christos H. Papadimitriou. On generating all maximal independent sets. *Information Processing Letters*, 27(3):119–123, 1988.

[48] Richard M. Karp and Vijaya Ramachandran. Parallel algorithms for shared-memory machines. In J. van Leeuwen, editor, *Handbook of Theoretical Computer Science, Volume A: Algorithms and Complexity*, chapter 17, pp. 869–941. North-Holland, Amsterdam, 1990.

[49] Richard M. Karp, Eli Upfal, and Avi Wigderson. Constructing a perfect matching is in random NC. *Combinatorica*, 6(1):35–48, 1986.

[50] Simon Kasif. On the parallel complexity of discrete relaxation of constraint satisfaction networks. *Artificial Intelligence*, 63(45):275–286, 1990.

[51] Dimitris Kavvadias and Martha Sideri. The inverse satisfiability problem. *SIAM Journal on Computing*, 28(1):152–163, 1998.

[52] Sanjeev Khanna, Rajeev Motwani, Madhu Sudan, and Umesh Vazirani. On syntactic versus computational views of approximability. *SIAM Journal on Computing*, 28(1):164–191, 1998.

[53] Sanjeev Khanna and Rajeev Motwani. Towards a syntactic characterization of PTAS. In *Proceedings of the Twenty-Eighth Annual ACM Symposium on the Theory of Computing*, pp. 329–337, Philadelphia, Pennsylvania, pp. 22–24, May 1996.

[54] Sanjeev Khanna and Madhu Sudan. The optimization complexity of constraint satisfaction problems. Tech. Note STAN-CS-TN-96-29, Stanford University, Stanford, CA, 1996.

[55] Sanjeev Khanna, Madhu Sudan, and Luca Trevisan. Constraint satisfaction: The approximability of minimization problems. In *Proceedings 12th IEEE Computational Complexity Conference*, pp. 282–296, 1997.

[56] Sanjeev Khanna, Madhu Sudan, and David P. Williamson. A complete classification of the approximability of maximization problems derived from Boolean constraint satisfaction. In *Proceedings of the Twenty-Ninth Annual ACM Symposium on Theory of Computing*, pp. 11–20, El Paso, Texas, 4–6 May 1997.

[57] Philip N. Klein, Ajit Agrawal, R. Ravi, and Satish Rao. Approximation through multicommodity flow. In *31st Annual IEEE Symposium on Foundations of Computer Science*, volume II, pp. 726–737, St. Louis, Missouri, pp. 22–24, October 1990.

[58] Philip N. Klein, Serge A. Plotkin, Satish Rao, and Éva Tardos. Approximation algorithms for Steiner and directed multicuts. *Journal of Algorithms*, 22(2):241–269, 1997.

[59] Hans Kleine Büning. Existence of simple propositional formulas. *Information Processing Letters*, 36(4):177–182, 1990.

[60] Hans Kleine Büning, Marek Karpinski, and Andreas Flögel. Resolution for quantified Boolean formulas. *Information and Computation*, 117(1):12–18, 1995.

[61] Dexter C. Kozen. *The Design and Analysis of Algorithms*. Springer-Verlag, Berlin, New York, 1992.

[62] Mark W. Krentel. The complexity of optimization problems. *Journal of Computer and System Sciences*, 36(3):490–509, 1988.

[63] Mark W. Krentel. Generalizations of Opt P to the polynomial hierarchy. *Theoretical Computer Science*, 97(2):183–198, 1992.

[64] Richard E. Ladner. On the structure of polynomial time reducibility. *Journal of the ACM*, 22(1):155–171, 1975.

[65] Leonid A. Levin. Universal problems of full search, *Problemy Peredachi Informatsii*, 9(3):115–116, 1973 (in Russian). *Annals of the History of Computing*, 6(4):1984 (in English).

[66] David Lichtenstein. Planar formulae and their uses. *SIAM Journal on Computing*, 11(2):329–343, 1982.

[67] Nathan Linial. Hard enumeration problems in geometry and combinatorics. *SIAM Journal on Algebraic and Discrete Methods*, 7(2):331–335, 1986.

[68] Richard J. Lipton and Robert E. Tarjan. A separator theorem for planar graphs. *SIAM Journal on Applied Mathematics*, 36(2):177–189, 1979.

[69] Richard J. Lipton and Robert E. Tarjan. Applications of a planar separator theorem. *SIAM Journal on Computing*, 9(3):615–627, 1980.

[70] Carsten Lund and Mihalis Yannakakis. The approximation of maximum subgraph problems. In Svante Carlsson, Andrzej Lingas, and Rolf G. Karlsson, editors, *Automata, Languages and Programming, 20th International Colloquium*, volume 700 of Lecture Notes in Computer Science, pp. 40–51, 1993. Springer-Verlag, Berlin, New York.

[71] Michel Minoux. LTUR: A simplified linear-time unit resolution algorithm for Horn formulae and computer implementation. *Information Processing Letters*, 29(1):1–12, 1988.

[72] Rajeev Motwani and Prabhakar Raghavan. *Randomized Algorithms*. Cambridge University Press, Cambridge, UK, 1995.

[73] Victor Pan and John Reif. Efficient parallel solution of linear systems. In *Proceedings of the Seventeenth Annual ACM Symposium on Theory of Computing*, pp. 143–152, Providence, Rhode Island, 6–8 May 1985.

[74] Christos H. Papadimitriou and Mihalis Yannakakis. Optimization, approximation, and complexity classes. *Journal of Computer and System Sciences*, 43(3):425–440, 1991.

[75] Christos H. Papadimitriou. *Computational Complexity*. Addison Wesley, Reading, MA, 1994.

[76] Christos H. Papadimitriou, Alejandro A. Schäffer, and Mihalis Yannakakis. On the complexity of local search (extended abstract). In *Proceedings of the Twenty-second Annual ACM Symposium on Theory of Computing*, pp. 438–445, Baltimore, Maryland, 14–16 May 1990.

[77] Christos H. Papadimitriou and Kenneth Steiglitz. *Combinatorial Optimization, Algorithms and Complexity*. Prentice-Hall, New York, 1982.

[78] J. Scott Provan and Michael O. Ball. The complexity of counting cuts and of computing the probability that a graph is connected. *SIAM Journal on Computing*, 12(4):777–788, 1983.

[79] Prabhakar Raghavan and Clark D. Thompson. Randomized rounding: A technique for provably good algorithms and algorithmic proofs. *Combinatorica*, 7(4):365–374, 1987.

[80] Stephen Reith and Heribert Vollmer. The complexity of computing optimal assignments of generalized propositional formulæ. Tech. Report TR 196, Department of Computer Science, Universität Würzburg, Würzburg, Germany, 1998.

[81] Walter J. Savitch. Relationships between nondeterministic and deterministic tape complexities. *Journal of Computer and System Sciences*, 4(2):177–192, 1970.

[82] Thomas J. Schaefer. The complexity of satisfiability problems. In *Conference Record of the Tenth Annual ACM Symposium on Theory of Computing*, pp. 216–226, San Diego, California, 1–3 May 1978.

[83] Alejandro A. Schäffer and Mihalis Yannakakis. Simple local search problems that are hard to solve. *SIAM Journal on Computing*, 20(1):56–87, 1991.

[84] Michael Sipser. *Introduction to the Theory of Computation*. PWS Publishing Company, New York, 1996.

[85] Larry J. Stockmeyer and Albert R. Meyer. Word problems requiring exponential time: Preliminary report. In *Conference Record of Fifth Annual ACM Symposium on Theory of Computing*, pp. 1–9, Austin, Texas, 30 April–2 May 1973.

[86] Larry J. Stockmeyer. The polynomial-time hierarchy. *Theoretical Computer Science*, 3(1):1–22, 1976.

[87] Seinosuke Toda. On the computational power of PP and $\oplus$P. In *30th Annual IEEE Symposium on Foundations of Computer Science*, pp. 514–519, Research Triangle Park, North Carolina, 30 October–1 November 1989.

[88] B. Trakhtenbrot. A survey of Russian approaches to perebor (brute-force search) algorithms. *Annals of the History of Computing*, 6(4):384–400, 1984.

[89] Leslie G. Valiant. The complexity of enumeration and reliability problems. *SIAM Journal on Computing*, 8(3):410–421, 1979.

Index